<u>Beyond Delmont Street</u>
<u>The High School Years</u>

By

Eric A. Mann
(Author of The Delmont Street Gang)

<u>Acknowledgements</u>

This book is dedicated to one grandchild, one girlfriend, and one "gang".

To my grandson, Nathan Mann: Although you're only eleven years old, I want you to know how much Mama and Papa love you, and how much joy you give us, every time you simply walk in the door.

To my wife, my "girlfriend", my partner and my best friend, Susie, I'm nothing without you. You've taught me what it means to be happy, loving and appreciative. After more than forty-five years together, I can't imagine what my life would have been without you. Your halo glows brighter every day.

Many thanks go to Amy Kellerman (WMOTN) for her artist's eye; the 1975 Manchester High School Yearbook Committee for the random photos from the SOMANHIS; and, to Stuart "Stuey" Flavell, for his insight.

Finally, my deepest appreciation and gratitude to everyone who bought, read and championed <u>The Delmont Street Gang</u>, and took the time to write a review, or send me a kind email, telling me how much you enjoyed the book; and, for encouraging me to do it all again. After all, at the end of the day, despite the tough veneer we may display, we all want to be liked and accepted…

…Just like in High School.

Foreword

So, here I am, dipping my toe into the writing pool, again. After I released <u>The Delmont Street Gang</u>, I started remembering other stories I could have included, and I was pissed! How could I forget that? And, this??? And, that???

But, then it dawned on me that I have enough material to write another book; to devote another three years of my life, writing and re-writing, toiling and slaving, and re-ENTERING THE EGO-CRUSHING WORLD OF MY OWN NEUROSES, AFRAID TO LET GO OF THE FINAL DRAFT, LIKE AN OVERBEARING MOTHER SOBBING OUTSIDE THE ELEMENTARY SCHOOL DOORS AS "JUNIOR" STARTS KINDERGARTEN…!!!!

…But, I'll be alright. Mom always said I would; because I'm special.

As we all know, life changes as you get older. We spread our wings, venture out, meet new people, and make new friendships. This is never truer as when you move on to high school. You start to take notice of the opposite sex, you join school clubs or sports teams and, generally, develop your own interests, which may not coincide with that of your childhood friends. This was certainly true for me.

I was a football player, a choir rat, and a musician; three things that most of my "Gang" really didn't do. Each of these would prove to introduce me to new friends who shared my interests and would remain a part of my life for years to come.

But this didn't mean that the Delmont Street Gang wasn't there; it just meant that we were being dragged in different directions, to explore new things, and to widen our individual social circles.

Hell, I have longtime friends who I have introduced to Karl and Larry Smith, Teddy Hanson and David

Corrado, who became friends of theirs, and vice versa. It just meant that we had surrounded ourselves with good people, and our numbers grew.

That's what this book is about; the stories outside of the neighborhood, and the adventures we would share. If you see yourself in these anecdotes, that makes things all the better. I received many emails and reviews regarding The Delmont Street Gang, from readers who were reminded of their respective childhood experiences. *"This could have been written about my neighborhood!"* was a constant statement. To that, I say GOOD! If DSG got your juices flowing, and motivated you to share your stories, that's a wonderful thing! I know of at least one person who has been actively writing about her neighborhood experiences, and I find myself laughing my ass off while reading her stories.

So, here's hoping that you enjoy Beyond Delmont Street, and that it reminds you of your years outside of your neighborhood, and you remember them fondly.

Holy Crap! I'm in High School!

If you went to Illing Junior High School, in Manchester, Connecticut, you had, depending upon your point of view, an advantage or disadvantage over the kids who attended cross-town rival Bennet Junior High. Why? Because the Illing ninth grade was housed at Manchester High. Why? BECAUSE THE ILLING BUILDING WAS TOO SMALL ON THE DAY IT OPENED! What the hell were our parents thinking?

So, you get my point! This was either an exciting time, or one which filled you with nothing but fear and anxiety. For me, it was exciting. I looked at it as an opportunity to, as my mom always reminded me, come into my own, to truly find out who I was. After all, I had BEEN through the anxiety and awkwardness of junior high, and this was like a complete do-over…

Or, so I thought!

At the time, Manchester High School was huge! A maze of classrooms, gymnasiums, fields and cafeteria, located at 134 East Middle Turnpike, and designed to intimidate even the most-courageous underclassman. And, the campus was OPEN! This meant we were treated like adults! We were able to come and go between classes, if we so desired! We could take a quick trip down to Burger Chef for lunch with your buddies, or a short car ride down to Dairy Queen for a Brazier. Personally, I loved it! Living two blocks from the campus meant that I could go home for lunch, if I wanted. If you were lucky enough to plan your schedule accordingly, you could actually have your afternoons off. During my senior year, my first class was at nine, and I was done before 1:00PM. It was a different time. We had more freedom. Parents weren't worrying about their kids getting into trouble.

But, there was one constant that I didn't consider. Just because you're in a different school does not mean you are allowed to start over. And, there are bound to be those "mean kids" who make sure that you can't. I don't think a day went by that some kid wasn't shoved into a locker, or some other kid would, for no apparent reason, smack some kid in the head, as he was passing in the halls. This was high school life; survival of the fittest. This was the seventies; specifically, 1971 through 1975. It meant long, unkempt hair, bell-bottom jeans, hip-huggers, clackers in the hallway, Zig Zag papers in your pocket (some, not mine…), Earth Shoes, cafeteria food, streakers, class trips, muscle cars, 8-track tapes, upperclassmen, underclassmen, going steady, breaking up, Friday night dances, football games on Saturday, "smoking on the hill", cheap pot, and weekend runs to the package store. And, because nothing ever changes from generation to generation, there was drama, drama, drama!

I guess my experience was no different than a lot of high school-aged kids. I was not one of the "Cool Kids", I didn't hang out with the "Stoners", and I wasn't smart enough to hang out with the "Nerds". I played football, but I didn't hang with the "Jocks". I was never invited to do so.

I was a "Choir Kid", so I guess that was my safe zone. But, I felt like an outsider there, as well. When I was an underclassman in the Roundtable Singers, our extracurricular choir group, someone who was a friend years before, made my life miserable; taunting me, and making sure that I knew that I didn't fit in. In fact, because of this "bully", I carried the nickname "Zero" for my first two years of high school. It almost caused me to quit singing. But, I learned to tough it out.

I'd like to think that I did a pretty good job of keeping my head on straight. I always tried to make those younger than me feel accepted. I didn't always succeed, but I sure tried. Bottom line, I knew how badly I felt by others cruelty, so I did my best to make the underclassmen feel accepted. Lord knows, I wasn't perfect. There was a kid whom I had known as far back as grade school, whom I had "bullied" during junior high. And, here I am, more than forty years later, and I still regret my actions. He didn't deserve that; no one does. So, I guess in some way, the teasing I endured in high school was my penance.

A few years ago, I had used the wonder of the internet to locate this "kid". I wrote a letter to him, profusely apologizing for my actions. I told him that I had never forgotten what I had done, nor had I ever forgiven myself. I just thought it was important that he hear it from me, directly.

I never received a reply; I didn't expect one. But, it was important to me that he knew I was sorry. Odds are, he had never given me a second thought, all these years later. And, I don't blame him. He's a better man than I.

And, while you're reading this, if I ever did anything to make you feel bad about yourself, I'm truly sorry. Chalk it up to being childish and stupid.

But, things did get better for me. I met other "Music Wing Kids" who would become lifelong friends; some, an integral part of my life. The Music Wing was comprised of a large rehearsal room for the Band Kids, a tiered rehearsal room for the choir kids, and about a half-dozen small practice rooms, each furnished with an upright piano, a couple of chairs, and a music stand for individual lessons and/or practice. This was my turf for a large portion of my day, when I wasn't in class. It was a place for serenity, reflection, and some quality "alone time". I would walk in on various choir classes, to join in the singing, or rehearse with the jazz band, or just grab a rehearsal room and plink away on the piano.

I used to love sneaking into an empty, dark Bailey Auditorium, just to get a bit of solitude, daydream about performing on that big proscenium stage, or even take a nap. I just loved being a part of that end of the school.

The cafeteria was on the south end of the school, almost directly across the parking lot from the music wing. Of course, like any other school, most of the daily socializing took place there, during lunch or free periods. I close my eyes, and I can still see the backgammon boards, card games, lunch trays, and cliques in the different corners. School spaghetti, salami grinders and my favorite, apple crisp!

The Brookfield Street parking lot promised a day of muscle cars, cigarette smoking, Frisbees, hanging out, and making plans for after school or the weekend. The school halls meant couples joined at the hip, making out between classes, socializing, hall monitors stopping the loitering or running, teachers hustling us all into the classrooms, and the occasional fist fight.

The Front Office meant handing in absentee notes, the nurse's office, daily student announcements, and punishment for the troublemakers (or, so I've heard…).

The Manchester High School property was huge, as high schools go. The front of the building faced East Middle Turnpike, and ran the entire length of Brookfield Street, past the football field, past the baseball fields, past the tennis courts, and ended on East Center Street. There were hundreds of places to get lost in on that property. There were miles of rain sewer pipes running under the athletic fields, which were explored regularly by hundreds of kids, including the Delmont Street Gang, despite of the fact that the pipes were overrun with rats.

At the back of the athletic field was a hill which, besides being used for running drills for the soccer and football teams, was used for a longtime unspoken tradition, where members of each year's graduating class would carve huge digits in the grass to represent their year. Our year was no different, as the hill bore what looked like a twenty-foot tall "75", carefully dug out and filled with white chalk dust. It was a matter of pride.

It was a bunch of kids just trying to make it through another year of school, and hoping that this was the year everything was going to be different; this was the year that everything would go right, popularity would be in reach, that cute girl or guy was going to pay attention, your skin was going to clear up, your grades were going to be better, you'd get the solo in the choir, you'd be a starter on the baseball team, and the nervous feeling in your stomach was going to disappear. We were all the same. It didn't matter who you were, how athletic, or how popular you were; we all had the same hopes, dreams and insecurities. And, it's a royal bitch. But, along the way, we all had some fun, and good memories.

After all, we were the Manchester Indians, the mighty, mighty Indians, and everywhere we'd go, people want to know, who we are, so we'd tell them…

… We were the Indians.

Illing & Bennet Football

There are some things about growing up that were hard to understand. For me, one was the transition from junior high sports to high school sports; especially football. I mean, COME ON, think about it! Illing Junior High and Bennet Junior High! Here we were, two crosstown rivals, beating the crap out of each other – hitting, punching, spitting, and whatever else we could get away with, and then we're expected to join together for the good of Manchester High, and play on the same team?!?

When I was in ninth grade, Illing met Bennet for the annual slugfest, at Mt. Nebo Field. It was a huge deal for all of us. Not only had our friends and family turned out, but Dave Wiggin, head coach for MHS, and a local "god", was there with the rest of his coaching staff, to get an idea of who would be joining the ranks of the mighty, mighty MIIS Indians.

I loved playing football. I had visions of playing college ball, then a career in the NFL. I thought I was on my way. I was six foot four inches tall, and about 190 pounds, and thought I would go all the way! I was truly pumped. I was determined to have a great game and inflict as much punishment on those bastards from the south side of town, as possible. I was starting tackle on both offense and defense. But, it was the defensive position which I relished. Hit, and hit, and hit.

Jack Maloney was the starting quarterback for Bennet. Although he couldn't have been much more than 5 feet 6 inches, he was a great athlete; a three-letter man in baseball, basketball and football.

Back then, long before trash talk was really on the radar, I was all about intimidation. Keep jabbering at your opponent, get inside his head; get him to show emotion, whether that meant making him mad, scared, frustrated, whatever. And, that's what I tried to do; get your opponent off of his game. Of course, it helped that I had a big mouth.

And, I was pounding the tackle across from me. Forearm shivers, slaps to the helmet, hooking under the back of his shoulder pads, and throwing him aside - just running all over him. And, at the same time, I would be harassing Jack.

I had caught up to him a couple of times during the game and sacked him. And, he was a pressure cooker ready to pop. Finally, in the last quarter, I broke through the line, and caught up to him, while he was back to pass. I grabbed him around the helmet, and took him to the ground, ripping his helmet off, in the process. Jack proceeded to lose him mind.

He jumped up, face beet-red, and started pushing me in the chest, and screaming at me. And, I shoved back. In the meantime, the Bennet head coach, Fred Lennon, charged onto the field, with Illing's Coach Heino close behind. Lennon ran over to me, grabbed me by the face mask, pulled me close, and growled:

"If you touch my quarterback one more time, I'm gonna sic my entire team on you!"

I was stunned! A coach! The OPPOSING coach, putting his hands on a player!?! I pushed him backward and broke his grip. Coach Heino got between us, and admonished Coach Lennon for his actions, and cooler heads prevailed. Coach Lennon returned to his bench.

The game ended without further incident. I truly do not remember which team won, but I can only assume that Bennet did, as Illing was not accustomed to winning. Coach Lennon came over, shook my hand, and apologized to me. All was forgiven. But, now the stage was set. How the hell were we expected to turn out for MHS football, and work as a team? We hated each other.

When "Hell Week" – two-a-day practices in the dead heat of summer – took place, the animosity was beat out of all of us, replaced by dirt, dust, dry heaving and salt tablets. Jack was there, I was there, and most of our teammates. Although I can honestly say that Jack and I were not friends, I would like to think we respected each other. At least I respected him. You'd have to ask him what he thought.

The point soon became moot, anyway. During Hell Week, I injured my wrist during fumble drill, and had to wear a latex cast for the rest of the season. That kept me on the Junior Varsity Squad, while Jack was Varsity. Then, I blew out my left knee, then my right knee. And, I STILL came back for more. That is, until I fell off of my bike after my junior year and separated my shoulder in three places. The doctor told me there would be no more football, ever.

So, I started a band.

The Jordans

During the sixties, there were not a lot of families of color in Manchester, Connecticut. Our neighborhood was all-white. The only African-American kids I knew were bussed to Bentley Elementary School.

One day, Mom brought a new friend to the house, and introduced me to Mrs. Eunice Jordan. Mom met Mrs. Jordan through their mutual friend, Anne Miller. The Jordans had recently moved to Mill Street, in Manchester's North End. Mrs. Jordan, her husband, Elijah, and their six kids (Gloria, Florence, Christopher, Ozzie, Doreen and Darlene) came to town from Queens, New York. It wasn't long before we all became fast friends.

Gloria was the oldest. She, and my sister, Jessie, were classmates at Manchester High School. Gloria was the total package – Gorgeous, smart, funny and sweet. Although she and Jess were close friends, Gloria and I found ourselves hanging out together on several occasions. She would pick me up in her grey Volvo sedan, and we'd go on road trips to Talcott Mountain, to lunch, or just to the Parkade Shops. We just enjoyed each other's company.

Florence was the second oldest. She had a sarcastic sense of humor, which I loved. Her catchphrase, to feign interest in whatever uneventful story was being told to her, was *"I'm happy for you"*.

Flo, as everyone called her, was responsible for initiating me into the African-American culture. She was the one who insisted upon "picking-out" my unruly mane of hair into a ridiculous white-boy Afro. I looked like I'd been electrocuted. It provided the Jordan family with some great laughs, though.

As Mr. and Mrs. Jordan were from the Colquitt County, Georgia, there was always a steady supply of real soul food. One day, while I was visiting their home, Flo was standing over the kitchen sink, washing something I'd never seen before.

"What the heck is that stuff?"

"Chitlins. You've never seen chitlins before?"

"In Manchester? Come on!" What are chitlins?

"Pig Intestines"

"Ewww! What are you doing to them?

"I'm washing the dookie out!"

"EEEWWWWW! I wouldn't eat that!"

"Good! You're not invited, anyway!"

But, there were soul food dishes that came out of that kitchen, about which I still dream, especially Mrs. Jordan's flapjacks with molasses syrup. I'm drooling, just thinking about them.

Flo also TRIED to teach me to dance with a little "groove". I remember being in their family room, with the Jackson Five on the stereo, with Flo and the other kids trying to teach me to dance the "Apple Jack". I looked like a spasmodic paraplegic. Again, I provided them great laughs.

Chris and Ozzie were the brothers. They were close in age with me, and we hung out a lot. We'd have sleepovers, play lots of baseball, build forts, ride bikes – all the things pals do.

Chris was into dirt bikes. He had a little Honda QA-50, and eventually upgraded to a 175 CC, and Ozzie inherited the smaller bike. One day, in the backwoods near the Jordan's house, the three of us went riding. Chris took his dirt bike and rode it up the side of this dirt hill, caught some air, and landed safely on the top. He then triumphantly turned to me and challenged me to do the same on the QA-50. Being a know-it-all kid, who was impervious to danger, or common sense, I revved the engine, and bore down on my intended target. I hit the path on the hill at full throttle, caught air, and the momentum from the back wheel pulled the bike right out from under me, causing me to land with a thud, right on my back, WITH MY FEET STILL ON THE PEGS OF THE BIKE, HOLDING THE ENTIRE WEIGHT OF THE MACHINE STRAIGHT UP IN THE AIR!!

I panicked! I knew that if my feet slipped off the pegs, the bike would come crashing down on top of me, causing untold injury.

> *"WHAT SHOULD I DO??? WHAT SHOULD I DO???"*
>
> *"Dump it on its side, man!"*

So, following Chris's advice, I leaned to one side, and let the bike topple to the ground, like a tree falling in the forest. I laid there for a minute, trying to compose myself. Chris and Ozzie ran over to me:

> *"You alright?"*
>
> *"Yeah, I'm okay."*

The brothers just looked at each other, shook their heads in disgust, turned and walked away.

> *"That was pitiful, man!"*
>
> *"Yeah! You'd better stick to walkin' Doofus!"*
>
> *"Give me a break! It was my first time!"*

"And, your last!"

Doreen and Darlene were fraternal twins. And, they became my sister Claudia's best friends. They were together an awful lot; either at one house or the other, at the movies, whatever. The most distinct memory I have of the three of them together, is when I walked into Claudia's bedroom, and found the three of them choreographing dance steps to the Osmond Brothers' "One Bad Apple". It still gives me nightmares.

All told, we were all tight. The families got together, my parents hung out with Mr. and Mrs. Jordan, and the kids all hung out with each other. And, more than fifty years later, we're still friends. Claudia sees Doreen and Darlene regularly. Unfortunately, living in Las Vegas has not allowed me to hook up with the Jordans in quite a while. But, through the miracle of Facebook, I stay in touch.

We lost Gloria, Flo, and Mr. Jordan over the years. Of course, my mom and dad are gone, as well. Mrs. Jordan was the last to go, in 2018. That was a sad day.

I'll never forget these wonderful people, and the great times that we had. To this day, it brings back warm memories. Right now, I'm thinking about Mr. Jordan, tooling around in his white Cadillac, with red leather interior, and I'm smiling.

They always make me smile.

The Girl Next Door

I had a crush – a MAJOR crush – on the "Girl Next
Door". Her name was Jane and she, along with her
mother, father, sister and brother, moved into the
neighborhood when she was twelve. I was thirteen, and
the first time I met her, my heart was playing the drum
solo from Inna Gadda da Vida. I was smitten.

She was gorgeous! Blonde hair, blue sparkling eyes, and
a killer smile. And, she was sweet. Most-importantly,
she was nice to me. These were feeling I had never
experienced before. Every time she was around, I was a
nervous wreck.

We started to hang together, as part of a relationship
that's built between neighbor kids. I would see her at our
house, playing with my sister Claudia, swimming in our
pool, or as part of a sleepover, organized by my sister.
Once in a while, I would be at their home, listening to

records, or playing some board game with Jane, and her brother and sister.

As we got a little older, it seemed as if she was interested in every other guy in the neighborhood, but me. For a while, she even dated David Corrado. As teenaged romances go, these were no different. A couple of weeks, maybe months, and that relationship would be over. When she and David broke up, I saw this as my chance. I asked her out. She turned me down, saying it was too soon. I was devastated. I mean, being fourteen at the time, and being shot down like that? It was tremendously traumatic. I worked up the courage to ask, and she wasn't interested. Ouch!

That didn't stop me from hanging out with her. But, as for me in her life I was meant to "worship from afar"; it would be nothing more. As time passed, I became, for lack of a better description, Jane's "Guardian Angel". If she'd have a problem with another guy, or there was some drama at home (and, there was a lot…), I was her "shoulder to lean on". I listened to her cry because some guy broke her heart, or her parents didn't understand her, I was there.

Her parents knew this, as well. Case in point – Fall of 1973 - It was after midnight, early Saturday. Manchester High School had held a dance in the cafeteria, on Friday evening. I had attended for a short while but had gone home early. As a sophomore, I just didn't feel like I belonged at these gatherings, which were overrun by upperclassmen.

I was in my room, watching television, when the phone rang in my parents' bedroom. This was unusual; a call after midnight? Who would be calling at this time of night, waking up my parents? Suddenly, Mom was knocking on the common wall between our rooms. This was the signal that the call was for me. WHAT???

I walked into Mom and Dad's room. Mom was holding up the receiver, toward me. In a half-asleep voice, Mom said:

"It's Mrs. Holder."

"Huh? Why is she calling me?"

"Something about Jane."

"Hello?"

"Eric, this is Mrs. Holder. Do you know where Jane is?"

"No. I saw her for a couple of minutes at the dance, but that was about eight o'clock."

"She hasn't come home, and we're quite worried."

"Have you gone to look for her?"

"No. We really don't know where to start. That's why I'm calling. Would you go look for her?"

"Why me? It's pouring rain, and it's after midnight."

"Please, Eric. You would have a better chance of finding her than anyone."

I was having mixed emotions; I was feeling used. I mean, this was their daughter, but they were too lazy to leave the comfort of their cozy home, and were asking me to search??? On the other hand, this was Jane. For better or worse, I couldn't leave her out there; she could be hurt. It was cold and wet. I had to go. I told Mrs. Holder that I would search for Jane and hung up the phone. Mom asked me what was going on. When I told her, all she could say in a tone of incredulity was *"Seriously??"*

I got dressed and headed out into the midnight rain. But first, a quick stop at the Smith's house. Sure enough, Karl was up, watching TV. I told him what was happening and asked him if he wanted to join me. He agreed. So, there we were, in the rain, walking up to the "scene of the crime", Manchester High School.

I had figured that, since the dance was in the cafeteria, we should start our search in the west side parking lot, which was directly adjacent to East Middle Turnpike, near the cafeteria entrance. A quick search by the cafeteria produced nothing. Then, we decided to walk around to the back of the school, by the tennis courts. A lot of "partying" was done on the hill on that side of the school, so that was as good a place as any to continue searching.

As we were heading toward the walkway, I had heard something by the trash dumpsters. In the darkness, I saw a form, on top of one of the trash receptacles. I walked closer; it was Jane, and she was very drunk, and soaked to the bone, and shivering. I combed the hair out of her eyes, and gently woke her.

"Janey, it me. Eric."

Jane opened her eyes, and immediately wrapped her arms around my neck, and collapsed in my arms.

"Eric, please take me home!"

I scooped her up, and the three of us started home. Along the way, Jane told me what had happened. Apparently, she had gone to the dance with an upperclassman, who had proceeded to feed her a considerable amount of liquor. And, when it didn't agree with her, and she became sloppy-drunk, he dumped her on top of the trash dumpster, to fend for herself. What a guy! There's a certain spot in Hell...

Along the trek to Jane's house, her arms wrapped tightly around my neck, her head on my shoulder, her looking like a drowned-rat mess, I was glad I had found her. As much as there was no romantic connection, I could not help but feel close to her. Why was it so easy to find her? It was as if there was always a connection. Jane didn't make things any easier on my emotions, as she proceeded to tell me that I was the only one who ever cared about her, and how I've always been there for her. I just chalked it up to her present state and knew that it would never turn into anything else.

Six blocks later, we arrived at the Holder's house. We walked into the back porch, and up the concrete steps, to the back door; Jane, still in my arms. Karl knocked on the door, and Jane's parents answered. I gently helped Jane to her feet. Her mother and father took one look at her, brought her into the house, shut the back door, and turned off the light. They never acknowledged that Karl and I were standing there; no thank you, nothing. In the dark, Karl and I just looked at each other, saying, in so many words, *"Can you believe that??"*

Time would go by. There would be no mention of our good deed by any of the Holders – no belated thanks, nothing. We weren't looking for gratitude, but you would think…

This would be the last time I was really a part of Jane's life. I would soon meet a girl who would capture my heart, and hold onto it for a long, long time. I would move on, and find new interests, and new friends.

And, Jane would become a memory.

I've Got a New Girlfriend

I've only had two girlfriends in my entire life. One, I dated for a short time while I was a sophomore, and then the last one I would ever have.

It had been a year since my first girlfriend and I broke up. It was way too much drama, caused by her weird home life, and her desire to escape. I was convinced that she wanted me to take her away from everything and, at the age of sixteen, I wasn't ready for that kind of commitment. So, I called it off, and remained single.

One evening, there was a house party near Bowers School. Karl Smith and I decided to attend, so we went stag. David Corrado was there with this cute, little brunette, whom I had never met. She was quiet and shy and, other than saying hello when David introduced us, stayed close to David the entire evening.

Of course, as the party progressed, I was too busy cutting up and having fun with the guys, as I usually did. David went outside to have a beer, and I struck up a conversation with his date. Her name was Susie. And, I could tell that she thought I was the strangest guy she'd ever met. After all, I was never one to try to play it cool. I liked being the class clown. Susie told me that she and David were just casually dating, and that this was actually their first time out. When David came back to the party, we talked for a while, and then Karl and I left.

A few weeks later, Susie and I were thrown together, again. As I was, once again, driving everyone to the Teen Center, David, Karl and I picked up Susie. While the guys were outside having a few cans of beer, Susie and I would talk. This would start to become a routine for the next few weeks.

Finally, when we were again left alone, we kissed. Actually, she kissed me (the hussy!). I guess she must have figured if she had to wait for me, it would never happen. It was just about then that David walked in the Teen Center and saw us cuddling in the corner. I didn't see him the rest of the night. I ended up taking Susie home.

The following morning, while I was sound asleep, my bedroom door crashed open. There stood David:

> *"Ya know, I'm not mad at you; I'm mad at her!"*
> *"Why?"*
> *"No girl breaks up with me!"*
> *"Whoa, whoa, whoa! There are a couple of facts you're not even considering!"*
> *"Like what?"*
> *"For one, you weren't even going steady. You told me yourself that you were just casually dating!"*
> *"Yeah? So?"*
> *"Two, what about all the girls you've actually dumped?"*
> *"Well, that's different!"*
> *"Why?"*
> *"It just is!"*
> *"Oh, fuck you!"*

That was the end of the discussion. David was cool with it. He realized that he had no real beef with either of us. He would move on to half a dozen other girls along the way. They loved him; and, why not? He's a sweetheart.

Over the next few months, there was nothing official between Susie and I; it was strictly casual dating or group activities. It just seemed like whenever I was going here or there, I'd call her up and ask if she wanted to tag along. As time went by, whenever I would be going out, I'd call her, nobody else.

Finally, I decided to make it "official". On April second, 1974, 17 days shy of her sixteenth birthday, I asked Susie to "go steady" with me.

Ironically, Sue's mom was none too happy. She loved David.

"Wake Up Little Susie"

"We've both been sound asleep,
wake up little Suzie and weep.
The movie's over, it's four o'clock,
and we're in trouble deep.
Wake up little Suzie, wake up little Suzie…"

- Written by Felice and Boudleaux
Bryant,
Performed by The Everly Brothers

So, Susie and I became an official item. The number one
rule, when dating a teenaged girl, is never piss off her
parents; and, I worked hard at that. I was polite,
respectful and adhered to the curfew set by Sue's mom. I
had built up a trust over the next several months, and her
parents felt more comfortable with me hanging around.
This was an accomplishment, especially when it came to
Ma Kearns. You see, she didn't want us to go steady in
the first place and gave Sue an ultimatum: *"If your*
grades start to slip, you can't go steady, anymore!"
Well, that didn't work, as Sue made the honor roll the

very next report card, and never dropped off. I was a *wonderful* influence on her (cough!).

Finally, we popped the "big question" to Susie's mom and dad. We asked if it would be okay to go see a Bruce Lee double feature at the Manchester Drive-In:

> *"Ohhh NO, You're not going alone to the drive-in!*
> *"Why not, Mom? We're just going to see Bruce Lee, and this is the only theater in which it's playing!"*
> *"Mrs. Kearns, I promise I'll have her home as soon as the movie is over."*
> *"That's NOT what I'm worried about! I know what goes on at drive-in theaters!"*

It was at this juncture, that Sue's dad, "Bucky", chimed in with what he thought was a logical counterpoint to Ma Kearns' objection: *"Oh, for chrissakes, Mary! If they wanted to fool around, do you think they'd need to go to the drive-in to do it? Leave 'em alone!"* Now, who could argue with that?

Ma Kearns finally relented, but not until after sternly looking directly at me, and saying: *"I'm trusting you with my daughter!"*

So, we went on a Saturday night, feeling quite grown up; our first drive-in date with no parents. We drove up the long drive to the ticket booth, where I purchased our student tickets, and drove to a strategically positioned parking spot, center screen, toward the front, but not too far from the concession stand. We were ready for an evening of badly-overdubbed Bruce Lee movies and some Walter Lantz cartoons, interrupted by a bevy of dancing hot dogs and poorly-acted commercials for the snack bar: *"What's to eat? What's to drink? Come on down to the snack bar, for your favorite goodies! Pizza! None better anywhere…"*

The movies started at around nine o'clock. That meant that I would have Susie home by a little after 1:00AM.

We watched the first movie, stretched our legs, went to the snack bar, and hunkered down to watch the second feature. That's the last thing I remember.

When I woke up, Sue was still sound-asleep. I looked around, and the place was empty. The work lights were on, and the only people there were the employees picking up trash around the lot! What time was it? I peered down at my watch, through glazed eyeballs…

IT WAS QUARTER AFTER TWO IN THE MORNING!!!! OH SHIT!!!! WE'RE DEAD!!!

I woke Susie up. She immediately went into panic mode. I quickly started the car, kicked up the dirt with my spinning tires, and careened out of the drive-in. The entire ride home, Sue was muttering *"Mom's gonna kill me! Mom's gonna kill me!"* I tried vainly to calm her down, knowing full-well that we were in big trouble. Our only hope was that Sue's mom and dad were sound asleep, and Sue could sneak into the house, and up to her room, undetected.

We arrived at Sue's house about twenty minutes later. I parked the car, and we tip-toed up the porch steps to the front door. The house was dark. Did we get lucky??? Susie turned the doorknob, and started to enter, when the door was ripped out of her hand! There, standing in the dark, in her bathrobe and curlers, was Ma Kearns! A shiver ran down my spine, as this tiny, but formidable figure stared at me with a menacing look. Susie immediately attempted to present her opening statement of defense: *"Mom, let me explain…!"*

That's all she had time to utter. Ma Kearns grabbed Susie by the arm, dragged her into the house, gave me one more bone-chilling glare, and slammed the door in my face.

I wouldn't see much of Sue for the next two weeks; she was on house lockdown, grounded. I would eventually have the opportunity to explain what had happened that night to Ma Kearns. Although she didn't totally let me

off the hook, I guess she believed me, because I'm here
to tell the story, today.

Teachers who Had an Impact on Me

Can you think of a more-thankless job in the entire world, than teaching; especially today???

Think about it. These days, when a kid brings home bad grades, the parents want to know what the teacher did wrong. Teachers are overworked, underpaid and unappreciated. It's sad, really. They deserve much better.

At the risk of sounding like the stereotypical "Old Guy", "In MY dayyyy", if we got in trouble in school, we got slammed at home. It didn't stop some of us from getting into trouble, but we knew there was a consequence. And, as difficult as this may be for some of you to believe, I too, got into mischief at Manchester High School (No, really! I did! Shocking, huh?).

But, that's not what this is about. I would like to tell you about the teachers who truly made a difference in my life at old MHS. They saved my high school career, academically and socially.

Vice Principal Larry Leonard makes the cut, because he, unlike some of his peers, was tolerant and understanding of this loud-mouthed, wise-cracking, underachieving student. Despite several visits to the Principal's Office during my sophomore and junior years, he never lost his temper. He always encouraged me to do better. He always told me that my best was yet to come, and I'd look back on all the nonsense, and wonder why I put myself through all of it. And, I believed him; and, he was right.

Lee Hay deserves a nod. He was a remarkable teacher; so remarkable, he would eventually be voted National Teacher of the Year. Not only did he teach English, he was in charge of Sock and Buskin, the extra-curricular drama club. They produced some very good plays, as high school drama clubs go. While I wasn't involved in S&B, it dawned upon me that Mr. Hay was fostering an atmosphere of acceptance, while encouraging the students' theatrical pursuits. I admired that; I admired the actors. To this day, I can't figure out why I wasn't one of them.

Adrian Groot was the Auto Shop Teacher. A mountain-of-a-man, he always seemed to be cool, calm and collected. He had to be; not only did he own his own station on East Middle Turnpike in Manchester, he dealt with six classes of knuckleheads every day. As you can imagine, he would teach us about auto repair, from the ground, up. Everything from oil changes, to tune-ups, to engine rebuilds. He was a master mechanic.

I was not Mr. Groot's best student. I received good grades and did the work; I was just not a born mechanic. What he did for me had a much-bigger impact than the classwork. You see, there were two notorious bullies in my class (who shall remain nameless, because they're not worth the attention, and are probably dead or in prison. But I digress…), and they thought nothing of making one's life miserable, especially if their target avoided any sort of fracas on campus. So, for the first few months of my senior year, they decided I would be their target. Every day, I would suffer the indignity of some insult, a threat, a push, a dirty look. I was intimidated.

Fast-forward to the holiday season. It was time for the annual MHS Holiday Concert, featuring all of the choir classes and the Round Table Singers, led by Miss Martha White, and the MHS Orchestra, led by Mr. Andrew Shreeves. Each year, during one school day, there would be a student assembly, where all classes were brought to Bailey Auditorium to see and hear our collective performance, which comprised of a cornucopia of holiday classics.

I was lucky enough to have been chosen to sing a solo during Roundtable's medley of "Good Christian Men Rejoice" and "God Rest Ye Merry Gentlemen". I was the soloist during "God Rest…" I was told I was very good. At least, that's what the "reviewer" wrote in MHS' school page, in the Manchester Herald newspaper…

Well, wouldn't you know it? I had auto shop, right after the assembly. And, like clockwork, the "bullies" started in, giving me all kinds of crap for singing; everything from "YOU SUCK!" to questioning my manhood, such as it was, at seventeen.

Just when I was starting to regret being there, and for standing out in a crowd, Mr. Groot blew his cork:

> *"Why don't you idiots just SHUT UP?!? You WISH you had as much talent as Mann has! Let's make a bet! Let's come back here in five years and see who's made the most out of his life; because I have a strong suspicion it's not going to be you two!"*

You could have heard the proverbial pin drop. Everyone was stunned; especially me. I had never had a teacher come to my defense like Mr. Groot had, that day. He saw an injustice and rescued me from it. A teenaged psyche is fragile enough; all the second-guessing and self-imposed embarrassment; and, he chose to do something about it. I had a new hero.

I walked a little taller, after that. For Mr. Groot had affirmed that I was doing something right; that I was appreciated. I never had the occasion to tell him what that day meant to me. I doubt if he would even remember it. After all, it was probably another routine day for a teacher at Manchester High School

But he made a difference. I hope he knows that.

Raymond Korbusieski was my twelfth-grade history teacher. He was a stout man, with a red, jowly face, and a flat-top haircut. He walked around between classes with a Muniemaker cigar in his mouth. Truth be told, he looked just like the army sergeant character, who always showed up in the Bugs Bunny cartoons.

It was the first day of my senior year. I had had an unremarkable sophomore and junior year, academically, just doing enough work to get by. I thought I was slick. "Korby" passed out his class syllabus and explained that we would have two chapters of reading per week, and class discussion. Over the weekend, we were to complete a two-page report on what we had learned in the past week. The paper would be graded and returned to each of us by Wednesday of the next week.

So, dutifully, I passed in two pages of words on Monday, figuring that teachers never actually read our homework. Wednesday came and, just before the end of class, Korby passed back our first two-page reports. And, I was SHOCKED! Nay, STUNNED! There, on my paper was a huge, red "F". I was PISSED! How DARE he give ME an "F"???

The bell rang, and my fellow classmates filed out. I remained behind, waiting to speak with my new nemesis. When I finally had Mr. Korby alone, I marched up to him, displaying all the indignation I could muster. "*Mister Korby, would you please tell me the meaning of this?*"

Mr. Korby looked at me with a half-smile, silently raised his index finger, as if to say *"One minute, please"*, walked over to the classroom door, shut it, locked it, pulled the window shade, and walked toward me, until we were virtually nose-to-nose. In a calm, but ominous voice which to this day, tightens my sphincter, he spoke:

> *"I know WHO you are, I know WHAT you are. And, if you think you're going to receive a passing grade by passing in CRAP like THAT, you're highly mistaken! You're a bullshitter, who thinks he's smarter than everyone else. Well, your charm isn't going to work, here. Earn the grade or fail! GOT IT???"*

I could barely move. I just stood there, slack-jawed and dumbfounded. He was on to me! The jig was up. I wasn't as slick as I thought. I muttered a half-hearted affirmative response, checked to make sure I hadn't shit myself, and got the hell out of there. I went home that afternoon and did quite a bit of soul-searching. It was time for a drastic change.

Things were extremely different for me from that day, forward. I truly realized that my behavior was stupid. And, as cliché as it sounds, I was only hurting myself. I decided to do the work in Mr. Korby's class, and every other class I had. And, it showed. I actually made the honor roll that quarter, and for the rest of the school year.

I loved Mr. Korby's class. Once I started to pay attention, I grew to truly love history. And, I raised my class rank over 100 places, just for doing the work. Funny, how that works…

A little side note about Mr. Korby's class; Susie had a free period, while I was in History. So, almost every day, she would walk with me to Mr. Korby's classroom, and spend a few precious moments with me, cuddling in the hallway, just outside the door. When the first bell would ring, signifying the start of class, a muscular arm would reach into the hallway, grab me by the ear, and drag me into the classroom. He'd look at Susie and tell her to take off. It became a running gag, which I remember fondly, to this day.

Fast-forward to the following September. Guess who Susie has for History??? Yep. Old Mr. Korby! When the bell rang, he marched into class, looked at the students, and screeched to a halt, as he locked eyes with Susie. He gave her a look of "Now, I've got you!" Of course, it was all in fun. She would love and respect Mr. Korby as much as I. And, she also got an "A".

Years later, I made it my mission to get in touch with Mr. Korby, as I wanted to tell him what an impact he had on my life. I found his son, Peter, living in Rockville, Connecticut. Peter told me that his dad had retired down south and gave me his address. I wrote to Mr. Korby and told him that I greatly owed him for the lesson he taught me. I wanted him to know that he truly made a difference. Although he never wrote back, I'd like to think that he appreciated hearing from me, and that someone noticed.

Every one of these teachers molded me, and my fellow students, at Manchester High School. And, for that, I will always carry gratitude, love and respect.

But, while we're on the subject of teachers, there is one missing from my list; one who affects me, and many others, to this day…

I Cry Every Christmas

I was walking in the snow, one night, and listening to
music on my I-phone. I pulled up "Christmas was Meant
for Children" and, after a few moments, stopped dead in
my tracks; I couldn't move. My thoughts immediately
rushed back some forty years ago, to Martha White, and
the Manchester High School Roundtable Singers.

Although Roundtable has been around for seventy-five
years, as far as I was concerned, the "Diamond Years"
were under the direction of Martha.

The wonderful feeling I and seventy students, who
devoted many after-school hours, used to get from the
concerts and rehearsals, and being one big family;
performing holiday concerts at senior citizens homes,
civic luncheons and, yes, even a funeral. We would
travel across the state of Connecticut, culminating in the
big finale each year – the Holiday Concert in MHS'
Bailey Auditorium, to the delight of our families and
friends.

I can still picture the evening rehearsals in the Choir Room; Tenors and Sopranos to the left, Basses and Altos to the right, Grand Piano in the front, and Martha conducting. I remember the "Cool Guys" not sitting in the conformed rows, instead turning their chairs sideways in front of the blackboards on either side of the room, so that some of the basses were facing some of the Tenors. I couldn't WAIT till I was a senior, so I could sit in this hallowed spot, and be cool.

I can still hear the standard, tried-and-true parody lines that worked their way into the lyrics of the songs, and were passed down year-to-year, class-to-class, such as in Robert Frost's Choose Something Like a Star: "...*tell us what elephants you blend. It gives us strangely lemonade...*"

Or, the Christmas classic, Do You Hear What I Hear. When we would sing the line *"Said the night wind to the little lamb…"*, and David Corrado would bleat out a perfect lamb impersonation:

"Mmmmmyawwwwwwh!", which would bust everyone up, but really piss-off Martha. She would BANG her hand on the piano, and bellow *"MIS-ter Cor-RA-do!"*, and proceed to scold David, while the rest of us were laughing our asses off, behind our sheet music. It became even funnier, when Brian Beggs learned to impersonate David, impersonating the lamb. We'd be dutifully singing the song, the lamb line would be sung, and Beggsie would let it rip…

"Mmmmmyawwwwwwh!"

(BANG!) "MIS-ter Cor-RA-do!"

And, we would lose our collective minds. Yeah, it was dumb and sophomoric, but we <u>were</u> dumb and sophomoric.

Martha took us to Hawaii for the first time in 1973, for a concert tour. I was a sophomore. We stayed at the Ilikai Hotel, on Waikiki. You might remember it from the opening credits of Hawaii Five-O, where Jack Lord, as Steve McGarrett, is standing on the balcony with the theme song rocking: *"duh duh duh duh duhhhh duhhhh…"*. Seniors Stan Wojcoski and Yogi Holmes took pity on me and let me share their room. ME, a lowly underclassman, rooming with two big shot seniors. Cooooool! That was the trip where I learned what a Mai Tai was, and to knock before entering a room. I also learned that when a bunch of us went on a bike trip to Hanauma Bay, I would be forced to carry all the snorkeling gear, as I had the only bike with a basket. How convenient! I remember sitting in the white sand inside a natural hole in the coral reef, and watching the waves roll over the top of us. Amazing! I remember Stan's maniacal laugh, as he would touch the sea anemones, and watch them recoil. Hilarious!

We would make the same trip in 1975. This time, I was the senior, sharing a room with Johnny Graff and David Corrado. Susie was on the trip, as well. While most of the kids were lying around the beach all day, she and I went everywhere, taking in as many sites as we could. To this day, we share a photo album which, when viewed by other "Rountablers", evokes the question: *"Now, where was I when you were going here?"*

One afternoon, Brian Beggs, Bruce Beggs, Bill "Bubba" Matthews and I rented a car, and drove up to Sandy Beach, on the North Shore, to swim. It was an overcast, stormy April day. But hey, we were experienced! We were veterans of Misquamicut Beach, in Westerly, Rhode Island. Days like this were a dime a dozen. So, we decided to go body surfing. The waves were pretty big; probably the biggest we had ever seen. And, here we were, four kids from little old Manchester in this picture-postcard locale, getting pummeled by the Pacific Ocean. It was a blast; and, we were the only people on the beach. It was all ours!

While we were in the water, a Jeep pulled onto the beach. Next thing we knew, a lifeguard, carrying a flotation buoy, was swimming out to us, and gave us a friendly greeting:

"How you guys doin'?"

"Fine! How are you?"

"Great! Do you know where you are?"

"Sure! Sandy Beach!"

"Right! Do you know what goes on here?"

"No. Not really."

"This is where we hold the Body Surfing Championships of the World."

"Wow! That's cool!"

"Do you know for what else this beach is known?"

"No. What?"

"It's known for the highest number of broken necks in the world! And, you guys don't belong out here; especially on a day like this!"

We looked at each other, as if to collectively say "oh shit", and decided to heed this valuable advice, and get the hell out. One-by-one, we reached the safety of shore. That is, everyone except Bubba. We didn't see him floundering, bobbing up and down, nothing. For what seemed like an eternity, we yelled for him; nothing. The lifeguard was ready to head back in for a rescue effort when, finally, a wave broke on shore, and there was Bubba, face down in the sand. We didn't move, waiting for a sign of life, when Bubba picked up his head, and spit out sand and water. He had been caught in the riptide and had done what every one of us had been taught for years by our dads - If you're caught in the undertow, tuck your body into a ball, don't fight, and wait to bob to the top.

We picked up our friend, piled into the car, and went back to the hotel. We had dodged a bullet, that day.

Speaking of Bubba Matthews, there's one Hawaii story which always cracked me up. On the day we had arrived at the Ilikai Hotel, we were ushered into a ballroom, where we were given an orientation about the do's and don'ts while we were there. The meeting was led by Hawaii Five-O star Al Harrington, whose job it was to try to keep us safe. One of the more-important issues Al spoke of was to avoid getting too much sun on the first day, stressing no more than fifteen minutes. I remember him telling all of us that we shouldn't be fooled by the cool tropical breezes; that the sun was brutal, and we'd get horribly burned.

Of course, there were a few kids who did not heed the warning. Three come immediately into mind; Cindy Tucker, Terry Sullivan and Bubba. They were all burned to a crisp! This was especially brutal for Bubba, as he was a blonde-haired, blue-eyed, pasty-skinned Irish kid

73

standing about 5-foot-five. Now, he looked like a stop sign with legs.

As I had said, we all bunked three or four to a room. Anyway, that night, poor Bubba was miserable; the pain from the sunburn was unbearable. The only way he was able to get any semblance of sleep was to wrap his entire body with wet towels, to stay cool. The following morning, the story goes that when he and his roommates had woken up, they were lounging in the room when the housekeeper, a feisty, little local woman, had come in to make up the room. Bubba was in the bathroom, when the maid went to make his bed. She felt the sheets and, finding them wet, barked out: *"Did that little runt wet the bed??"* His roomies busted up, while Bubba tried in vain to explain about his burn, and the wet towels. I wonder if she believed him.

The most-sobering moment of the trip was our visit to Pearl Harbor, and the Arizona Memorial, site of one of the most-tragic moments in American history. We were standing on top of the resting place of 1,102 sailors and Marines. You could hear a pin drop.

Something compelled Miss White to gather us together and have us sing "Let There Be Peace on Earth" for the memories of these men, the other tourists, and for ourselves. To put it mildly, the tears were flowing. It was the most moving, and one of the hardest privileges a bunch of kids from Manchester, Connecticut would ever have. I think if you were to ask any one of them today, they would say the same thing.

The annual MHS Musicals – Hello Dolly, Unsinkable Molly Brown, My Fair Lady – those were the three during my years there. None of my favorites, but we had fun, anyway. We would have the same, tired choreography *("Diamond Step, everyone!")* every year, with the boys in a kick line, which would bring the audience to its feet. And, our parents were so proud to see us onstage, no matter how small the role. And, you never knew what stunts would be pulled during each production; like spiking one of the main character's beer mug with rum, on opening night (Not me! I didn't do that!).

On graduation day, June of 1975, I would sing with Roundtable one final time. We were part of the graduation ceremony. There we were, with our caps and gowns, intermingled with the Roundtable underclassmen left to carry on the legacy the following year. It was truly bittersweet. When we had completed our last song, the graduating seniors had to return to their respective seats with our fellow seniors. As I was leaving the risers for the last time, I stopped in front of Martha, and hugged her, without exchanging words. I couldn't have spoken even if I had wanted.

But I wanted her to know what she meant to me; to everyone.

These were shared experiences by a bunch of kids who may have never had the opportunity, were it not for Roundtable; experiences that, once high school was over, some would never experience again, only to return to the confines of their lives in Manchester, with only faded memories of a time when, in some little way, we were a part of something bigger than all of us, something that gave each of us an identity.

While I was remembering these moments, I just stood there, and looked up at the sky. My chest heaved, and I cried; tears of sadness <u>and</u> joy. I miss it. I miss it a lot – not for longing of a past glory, but for its purpose, its friendships, its support system, its good tidings…

…Its leader. And, for the lifelong memories she gave us. We could have/should have appreciated it more, at the time. But we were kids. And, regret doesn't always set in, in time to make amends.

I spoke with Martha for the last time, around 1987. I was living in Burbank California; Martha was living with her "cousin" Charlotte Whyte, in Laguna Niguel. She had terminal Cancer. She was in good spirits and said *"Tell everyone back home that I love them, and I'm going to beat this!"* I actually told her that I loved her and started to cry. And <u>she</u> comforted <u>me</u>.

Martha died a few weeks later.

I'm not ashamed to say that I'm crying, while I'm writing this. I have to stop every so often to wipe my eyes, because it's hard to see the computer screen. I've never shared this with anyone. But I'm glad I have. Because, if I'm not wrong, there are hundreds of RT members out there, who feel much the same as I do. It was a wonderful time, a wonderful experience, and only a very lucky few have the privilege of sharing these memories, and proudly say *"I was a Roundtable Singer."*

And, we owe <u>that</u> to Martha.

The Wallet

As I had previously stated, when you're dating, "Never piss off the parents". I cannot stress this rule enough.

Susie and I were, once again, on a date. And, there happened to be a television show which we wanted to see, very badly. As her house was closer than mine, we sped to the Kearns residence. I parked the car in front of the house, we ran up to the front door, and blasted into the living room. There was Sue's dad, "Bucky", watching TV.

> *"Dad, there's a show we want to see! May we turn the channel?"*
> *"I'm watching my program!*
> *"Please Dad! We can't miss this!"*

Bucky was resolute about not leaving his "Comfy Chair": *"Go up to my bedroom if you wanna watch it!"*

So, we ran up the stairs, turned on the tube in Bucky's room, and flopped on the bed, just in time to see the opening credits. Whew! We didn't miss it!

After the show, Susie walked me to my car, we called it a night, and I went home to bed. The following day while preparing to go out, I realized that my wallet was missing. Where could I have lost it? Parkade Bowling Lanes? Harry's Pizza? I had no idea! And, no one had turned it in at either establishment. Dammit! Now, I'd have to cancel my credit card, replace my license, the whole shmear! This is never a fun process, but it had to be done. So, I was off to the DMV office in Wethersfield to spend two-plus hours in line to get a replacement license.

Time passed. About six months later, I was invited to Susie's for Sunday dinner. I always looked forward to Ma Kearns' Sunday dinners, as she always put on the proverbial "feed bag"; it was almost as good a spread as Thanksgiving, which she also "did to the nines". Baked ham, potatoes, veggies, homemade pie –the works! And, as it was obvious that Susie wasn't going to get rid of me anytime soon, I was becoming a regular at the table, along with her sister Linda, and her brothers, Steve and Sean. These meals were fun. They were a lot of laughs, family and arguments, usually Steve and Bucky jawing at each other about one topic or another, while Sean was providing background music: *"OH YEAHHHH, Kool-Aid's here, bringin' you fun…"* It was mayhem, and I loved every one of them.

We were all sitting at the table, waiting for Ma Kearns to start serving it up, when she slowly, deliberately walked into the room, looking none too happy. And, she was staring daggers right at me! What did I do??? And then, with an accusatory tone which could only be mustered by a protective mother, she spoke: *"Young man, do you mind telling me why I found THIS under myyyyyy BED???"*

And there, in her right hand was my long-lost wallet! My mind started racing! My pulse quickened! I was dripping flop sweat, as I tried to utter an explanation, but could only muster a poor imitation of Ralph Kramden: *"Hamina, hamina, hamina..."*

That's when Bucky came to my rescue: *"Oh, for chrissakes, Mary! Leave the poor kid alone! He probably dropped it under the bed when he and Susie were watching TV! I told them to go up there!"*

It all came rushing back! That's exactly what happened. Ma Kearns softened a bit, sighed, handed me my wallet, and sat down to Sunday dinner. But it seemed as if every time I would look over at her, she was giving me that menacing look, and thinking *"I'm watching you, boy!"*

I never darkened the door of her bedroom, again. To this day, I'm afraid to go in there.

The Amazing Kreskin Gets Duped

THIS was an embarrassing episode for Manchester High School. No getting around it, the perpetrators must truly regret their actions to this day.

The Amazing Kreskin, the world-renowned mentalist, who was a regular on just about every talk show on the planet during the seventies, was appearing at Bailey Auditorium at Manchester High School. He would "amaze" the sold-out crowd with his feats of mind reading, telepathy, and the like, while the audience ate it up!

His final trick before the intermission would go down in infamy, as the day that Kreskin was scammed out of his paycheck by a couple of teachers, and an unwitting student.

The setup was this: Kreskin made an announcement to the crowd that he held his paycheck, for the evening's performance, in his hand, while holding it aloft for all to see.

He asked for volunteers from the audience to assist him with this display of mental acuity. Two well-known teachers, and an MHS student, who were involved with the organization of this event, would assist Kreskin.

Kreskin explained that he would step out of the building, while the three "assistants" would hide the check somewhere in the auditorium. Upon his return, and with the assistance of the MHS student's concentration, he would attempt to discern the location of the hidden check.

While Kreskin was escorted from the auditorium by one of the teacher-assistants, the other eagerly whispered some instruction in the student's ear. The student gave the teacher a look of puzzlement, but acquiesced. The two of them walked halfway up the aisle of the auditorium and hid the check in a female audience member's shoe. Then, they walked to the front of the audience, and awaited Kreskin's return.

When Kreskin reappeared, his instructions to the student were for her to take his arm, and to concentrate as to the whereabouts of his hard-earned fee. The demonstration started.

Over the next several minutes, Kreskin acted very strangely; walking in multiple tight circles, wandering out to the parking lot, up and down the aisles, while muttering something along the line of *"I don't understand this! Why do you have me walking in circles? Why are we going to the parking lot? The check was supposed to remain in the auditorium!"*

There was very little laughter from the crowd, while the discomfort level rose, demonstrably. All the while, the "Whispering Teacher" was having quite a giggle. After what seemed like twenty minutes. Our embarrassed guest threw his hands in the air, and stated: *"Ladies and gentlemen, this is the first time in my career that I have been unsuccessful in retrieving my fee. I'm very sorry; I've failed."*

It was at this time, that the "Whispering Teacher" divulged the ruse he was playing on Kreskin, and that he had instructed the student to take the mentalist on a wild goose chase. Kreskin's face dropped, as he attempted to muster his dignity, while reacting to the situation: *"Well, the joke's on me! I guess you win, and I lose! Ladies and gentlemen, I'd like to take a short intermission, before continuing. We'll be back in fifteen minutes."* With that, Kreskin marched backstage, with the contingent of "assistants" following close behind.

I wasn't privy to what transpired during that intermission, but the version going around town was that Kreskin lit into the assistants, in a very heated manner. And, who could blame him? They embarrassed him at his workplace. The show organizers pleaded with Kreskin to take his check, but he refused, telling them that he had never been treated so shabbily in his life.

When the audience had returned to their seats, and the lights went down, Kreskin returned for the remainder of the show; but, not before having the "final say". He calmly told the crown that he was the victim of a poorly timed joke, which ruined his chance for success. He also stated that he was forfeiting his fee and would not be returning to Manchester High School. The audience was not happy. Collectively, we felt horribly for what had happened, and also felt as cheated as Kreskin. We paid to see a complete show, not some pinhead's attempt to steal the spotlight. A smattering of boos and catcalls emanated from the audience. Cries of *"Give him his money"* could be heard. Kreskin calmed the crowd and continued for what was a half-hearted attempted to give us the remainder of the show. Then, it was finally over.

Over the next several days, there was a feeling of unease around the halls of MHS. Rumors abounded, complaint calls came into the school, and speculation rose. But nothing really happened, after that, Not that I ever heard about, anyway. Life went on, things went back to normal, the "Whispering Teacher" had a nice, long career at MHS, and the memory faded away.

A few weeks later, Kreskin appeared on the <u>Mike Douglas Show</u>. He took this opportunity to tell the United States viewing public that he had been ripped off during a visit to Manchester, Connecticut. Mike Douglas was appalled. The other guests were, likewise. When asked if he would ever return to do another show in Manchester, Kreskin replied: *"Not in THIS lifetime!"*

So, what's the moral, here? Stick to teaching, dumbass! Stay out of show business!

Henry

This is a controversial story. Some of you will believe, while others will tell me that I'm full of crap. And, that's okay; I've dealt with the skeptics for years; people who have said "I have never experienced it, so I don't believe in it'. To them I have one question – Do you believe in God, and have you seen him?

We lived at 255 Summit Street, in Manchester, near the corner of Hollister Street, in a two-story colonial. There was nothing out-of-the-ordinary about this house, other than the family who lived there. It had four bedrooms. If you were to climb the stairs to the second floor, you would find Jessie's bedroom to the left; her room facing Summit Street. Claudia's room was to the left, at the back of the house. Mom and Dad's room was to the right, facing Summit Street, and my room was at the back of the house. I shared a common wall with my parents' room. In fact, if you removed the common wall, Dad and I would be sleeping head-to-head. It's important that I explain the layout to you, as it will help to explain the following story.

Although it didn't make sense to me at the time, the first "close encounter" I recall was when I was no more than eight years old. Jessie would have been twelve, and Claudia, six. Jessie had a queen-sized bed, handed down from Mom and Dad. It had a carved wooden head and foot board and, on occasion, the three of us would sleep together in that bed. I would always sleep on the outside, as I tended to get up at night, to use the restroom. We would talk and laugh, until we dozed off. The bedroom door was always left open, so Mom could hear us, on the other side of the house.

One night, I woke up, and looked toward the bedroom doorway. In the dark, I made out the figure of someone standing there. I called out, in a half-whisper:

"Mom? Dad? What's the matter?"

But there was no answer. Whoever it was, walked toward the other side of the house. So, I assumed it was one of my parents, not wanting to wake everyone up. So, I went back to sleep.

The following morning, I asked my parents why they didn't say anything, when they came in to check up on us:

> *"What are you talking about? We never came in to check up on you!"*

I guess that it was about this time that Jessie started to have night terrors. She would wake up in the middle of the night, screaming at the top of her lungs. The first couple of times, it was frightening; but, after a while, I was just annoyed:

> *"Will you SHUDDUP?!?"*

Mom would run in to console her, and I would drift back to sleep, clueless to the real reason for Jessie's distress.

Over the next couple of years, there were other incidents that I had experienced, but never made a connection; like the dog barking at nothing, seeing something move out of the corner of my eye, yet nothing was there; things like that.

One Sunday evening, the whole family was in my parents' room, watching Ed Sullivan. I wasn't feeling particularly well, so I decided to go to bed. I said goodnight and went to my room. Through the common wall I could hear my family talking and laughing at the lineup of acts, as I started to doze off. I was lying on my right side, getting closer to a sound sleep, when I started to hear a noise; it sounded like someone impersonating a grandfather clock, by clicking their tongue on the roof of their mouth. I turned my head toward the noise, and there, floating over the foot of my bed, was an apparition, from the waist-up! I could see dark hollows for its eyes, nostrils and mouth, which was clicking away, like the clock I had heard! A total rush of terror took over my body, and I screamed at the top of my lungs! Dad came crashing through my bedroom door, yelling into the darkness:

"GET THE HELL OUTTA HERE!"

Mom was right behind him and flipped on the lights. I was freaked out!

"MOM! WHAT'S GOING ON? WHAT'S HAPPENING???"
"I guess it's about time we told you."
"TOLD ME WHAT??"
"We have a ghost."
"WHAT DO YOU MEAN WE HAVE A GHOST?? YOU <u>KNEW</u> ABOUT THIS, AND DIDN'T THINK IT WAS IMPORTANT ENOUGH TO TELL ME???"
"You're the only one who didn't know. You were the only one getting any sleep; so, we figured you'd find out, soon enough. So, why upset you, needlessly?"

"IS THIS WHY JESSIE HAS BEEN HAVING NIGHTMARES?"

"Yes."

"AND, EVERYONE HAS SEEN IT?"

"EVEN CLAUDIA?"

"Yes. She calls him Henry."

"WHAT DO YOU MEAN SHE CALLS HIM HENRY???"

"Well, he has visited her, and she talks to him."

Holy shit! I was dumbfounded. Mom and Dad stood there, with a look of helplessness on their faces. I mean, what could they do? This was the late sixties. What did anyone know about ghosts, or help getting rid of them, for that matter?

Now that I knew what was going on, the sightings were sporadic. Either I was a very sound sleeper, or "Henry" wasn't making himself available to me. However, there were a couple of major incidents which took place, along the way. One time, when I was twelve, on a very cold winter evening, Mom, Dad and Jessie were out, while

Claudia and I were home alone. I asked Claudia if she minded if I went over to the Smith's house for a while. She didn't, so I went. About an hour later, Dad calls the Smith house, and tells me to come home, immediately. He was pissed. He and Mom were visiting their friends, the Burgesses, when Claudia called them, in hysterics. "Henry" chased her out of the house and, when my parents got home, Claudia was standing in the driveway, in the snow, wearing her flannel nightgown. He laid into me, admonishing me for leaving my little sister home alone, and being irresponsible. I felt terrible; the fear on Claud's face made me feel like a heel.

Another time, Mom, Dad and Claudia went to Cape Cod, for a short vacation. Jessie and I didn't want to go. I was thirteen, and Jess was seventeen. Our parents trusted us and allowed us this grown-up freedom. I had gone out to play baseball, and Jess was gone, who knows where? After several hours, I came home, walked in the back door, and found the kitchen faucet turned on, full blast. The water had overflowed, and had worked its way into the living room, the dining room, and was cascading down the basement steps. I panicked! After turning off the faucet, I went downstairs to survey the damage. The basement was flooded with about two inches of water. I was by myself. I had no idea how to handle this! So, I called the one person I know I could count on; one of the few grown-ups who was cool, upon whom I could depend, my Uncle John.

John Davids was, and always would be, my uncle, despite the fact that he was divorced from my Aunt Adele (Mom's sister). He and Adele produced two children, Heather and Kevin, who were my closest cousins. Hell, Kevin was, and is, like the brother I never had. Anyway, everybody loved John. He was a tall, jovial guy, with bright orange hair. He was the King of the Gingers. John introduced me to music to which I had never thought of listening, including Buck Owens and Glen Campbell. As a musician himself, he took great joy in the fact that I was pursuing music, and he actually came to see me perform with one of my many garage bands.

When I told him what had happened, he came right over, no questions asked. First, we mopped up the kitchen, living room and dining room. Then, with a couple of milkshake cups, courtesy of Iona Appliances of Manchester, Uncle John and I spent the next several hours bailing out the basement. When I told him who, or what, I thought had caused this, he looked at me as if I'd gone over the edge. But he never left my side. He even left it up to me as to whether I would tell Mom and Dad what had happened. I did tell them, and they believed me. Well. Why not? That was just a part of the weird crap that had gone on.

Another time, Dad and I were in his room, watching television. No one else was home. All of a sudden, we heard the sound of glass breaking, emanating from Jessie's room. The two of us jumped up to investigate. Upon turning Jessie's bedroom light on, there, in the center of her floor, was her antique vanity mirror, lying face down. We lifted it up, but the glass was intact. Now, this was strange, in and of itself, as this mirror was held onto the wall by a very large nail, and a very thick strand of woven frame wire. The nail was still in the wall, and not one perfume bottle was out of place. So, how did the mirror get down off the wall, and what caused the sound of breaking glass?

It was about this time that I had caught wind of a pungent, petroleum odor. Across the room, diagonally from the vanity, at a distance of about twelve feet, was one of Jessie's perfume bottles, smashed through the center of her kerosene lamp; and the kerosene was running freely on top of her dresser. Dad and I just looked at each other, both realizing what had happened.

One time, Jessie decided to have a house party, in our basement. There were about twenty kids in attendance. Sometime during the course of the evening, some pinhead came up with the brilliant idea to have a séance. Jessie repeatedly begged them not to play around. Of, course, they didn't listen. She ran upstairs to tell Mom. Mom opened the basement door and yelled down to the party: *"You kids better knock it off! I don't want you messing around, like that!"*

One of the smartass teenaged boys retorted: "Ooooooh! Is the ghost going to come and get us?"

No sooner had the mental midget finished his disrespectful remark, when someone, or something SLAMMED him in the side of the head, knocking him to the floor. The entire basement emptied in a REAL hurry, and the party was over.

One of Jessie's friends, named Gina, was having trouble at home, and asked if she could stay with us. Mom had no problem with Gina staying with us; she could always use the basement for her bedroom, but Mom warned her that she might see "something". Gina scoffed, telling Mom she would be fine, and moved into our basement.

The Mann Family basement was paneled in real knotty pine wood; so real, I took great joy in knocking out a few knots, to make spy holes. On the other side of the basement, behind the knotty pine, was our furnace/laundry/storage room. Gina slept on our foldout couch, which was covered in thick, green vinyl, and had wooden arm rests. If you pulled out the bed, put down some sheets, prop up some pillows, it was damned comfortable. Many times, I would nap on it, when I just wanted to get lost. At the foot of the bed/couch, and another five feet beyond, was a knotty pine box shelf, which was built to cover an old utility sink. On top of the shelf was a 19-inch television.

One night, after everyone had gone to sleep, Gina was lying in bed, reading a book. Over the top of the book, something caught her eye. There, in the turned-off television, was the blurry figure of a man, with his arms folded, staring at her. Gina chalked it up to her imagination, and turned off the light, to go to sleep. Shortly thereafter, something GRABBED her by both legs, and started turning her over and over, in the bed! Gina ran upstairs, through the kitchen, up the stairs to the second floor, screaming the whole way! Mom and Dad woke up and spent the next several hours consoling her.

Gina moved home, the next day.

We were over this! How much more were we expected to take? We couldn't live our normal lives because this poltergeist was having too much fun, causing havoc! Something had to be done, but what?

It was the summer of 1971. There was a special event being held at Bailey Auditorium, at Manchester High School, and Mom and Mrs. Haley decided to attend. This was something new; something Manchester had never seen before. This was a lecture about ghosts, demons, hauntings and exorcism, presented by two of the pioneers in the field of ghost hunting, Ed and Lorraine Warren. Now, the Warrens had built quite a reputation in helping to "cleanse" homes of spirits. Their work has been documented for years. As a matter of fact, they were the ones called in to handle the Amityville Horror house. But Lorraine was so freaked out by the evil this house held, they quit the job. It's covered in the book of the same title. Ed and Lorraine's exploits were also the fodder for the recent "Conjuring" movies.

Their presentation included super-8 footage, stills and audio recordings. Remember, this was well-before VHS tape. The Warrens enthralled the audience with two hours of chills and thrills. At the end of the show, they stayed to sign books, and answer questions from the audience. Mom wanted to meet them and was standing in the throng encircling Ed and Lorraine, about ten feet away. It looked like it was going to be a while to meet them, if they didn't call it a night, beforehand. But a funny thing happened, while Lorraine was talking to someone at the front of the pack. Lorraine kept becoming distracted, and turning her attention toward Mom, for no apparent reason. Lorraine would regain her concentration and continue her ongoing conversation. Then again, she became distracted, and looked right at Mom. Finally, Lorraine's curiosity got the best of her. She excused herself from the conversation she was having, and made a beeline through the crowd, and stood face-to-face with Mom, and said in a very soothing voice:

"You have a problem at home, don't you?"

"How did you know?"

"I don't know. You're just giving me a strong feeling that you need our help."

Tears welled up in Mom's eyes. Now, if you knew my mother, you would know this was no easy trick. My mom was one of the toughest, most-ballsy women I've ever met. But she was tired of this, and relieved that, finally, someone truly understood, and wouldn't look at her as if she were ready for a padded room (At least not for this!).

It was about ten-thirty on this same, warm summer evening. I was standing in our kitchen, when the back door opened. In walked Mom, Mrs. Haley, and two people I had never met before.

"Eric, this is Ed and Lorraine Warren."

"Nice to meet you. Wait a minute, aren't these the people…"

"Yes. We just came from their lecture. They want to help with our situation."

Holy crap! I knew about these guys! I heard the stories; Amityville, all that! And, they're here? Freaky! The Warrens asked if they could see Jessie's room. So, we all headed upstairs. I showed the Warrens Jessie's bedroom, and Lorraine glided into the room, with Ed close behind. Lorraine slowly walked about, stopping at several points, using her hands as if she were trying to feel something in front of her that wasn't there. Finally, she walked into the open closet. Mom, Mrs. Haley and I were all watching, as we saw Lorraine's breath, as she exhaled. Although the temperature was well into the eighties, Jessie's closet was cold; very cold.

"This is the origin of the spirit. This is where it draws its energy. Do you have something of Jessica's that I may take with me, tonight? It will help me to focus on the energy and gain a better idea of exactly what we're dealing with."

Mom told her to take whatever she wanted. Lorraine ended up taking a couple of those big, pink hair rollers girls used to use. It was then that Ed and Lorraine said they would be back the following night, to continue their investigation, and perform a séance (Side note: Why always at night? Can't this be done in broad daylight?). They asked that Mom, Jessie and I be available to participate. The Warrens assured us that they would handle this, and that everything would be alright.

The following evening, the Warrens were back. We had set up a card table, with five chairs, in the center of Jessie's room. Mrs. Jordan had come over to visit Mom, unaware that all this was going on; and, she was not very comfortable with it. But, she stayed, and was watching television with Dad and Claudia, in my parents' bedroom.

Jessie and I sat across from each other, at the table. Mom sat to Jessie's right, Ed was on one end, and Lorraine on the other. Ed explained what would go on, how he would ask questions of the spirit, while Lorraine would answer

– not in some possessed voice; just her normal voice. She was the "conduit".

So, we started. And, it was much like every séance you've seen in a dozen movies; everyone holding hands, darkened room, except for candlelight, and Ed calling out to the spirit world. It was just another average evening in the Mann household.

Meanwhile, Dad, Claudia and Mrs. Jordan were still in my parents' bedroom, when Claudia says, very matter-of-factly:

> *I don't know what they're doing in Jessie's room, but it's not working!"*

> *"Why do you say that?"*

Claudia pointed toward the corner of the room:

> *"Because he's standing over there!"*

Mrs. Jordan started to freak out! The family dog was staring at nothing, fixated on the same spot to which Claudia had pointed. All of a sudden, Claudia and the dog started turning their heads, following "nothing" as it left the room.

"He's leaving, now."

It was about this time that things started happening at the séance. Jessie's head tipped forward, as if she had fallen asleep. While I'm staring at her, the sleeve of her sweater started pulling away from her body, by itself, over and over; as if someone were 'plucking' it! Now, I'm officially scared out of my mind. But I kept my composure. Mom too, was fairly composed.

It was about this time that Lorraine acknowledged that the spirit had joined us, and she and Ed started a question-and-answer session. Ed asked: *"Why are you here? Why this family?"*

To which Lorraine, speaking for our visitor, replied:
"Why not?"

"How did you get here?"

"I followed the girl home from the cemetery"

"What cemetery?"

"East Cemetery."

"Don't you know that you don't belong here? Don't you know that you no longer belong in this world?"

(silence)

"It's time for you to go on your way, to be with the others who have left this world, as well. You've had your time in this physical world, and it's time for you to move on, and stop frightening these people."

(silence)

Ed tried for the next several minutes to get a response, to no avail. Soon, Jessie raised her head, and looked around as if nothing had happened. Lorraine told us the spirit had gone. The candles were blown out and the lights turned on.

Lorraine started to tell us that this was a male spirit, from the late 1700's, dressed in period clothes, and none too happy to be deceased. She asked Jessie about the "East Cemetery" reference. Jessie surmised that the "attachment" happened as a result of the Bentley School field trip, where her class would create gravestone rubbings, by putting a piece of onion paper over the stone, and rubbing it with charcoal, to capture the image. At the time, this was a standard field trip.

Ed and Lorraine were convinced that Henry was gone. But, in the event that he would show up again, we were to declare "In the name of God, leave this house, and leave us alone!" The Warrens left, and we felt much safer.

A few months had passed, and everything had returned to normal, or as normal as it could be, around the Mann house. I was always the last to leave the house, every morning. Mom and Dad to work, Claudia and Jessie to school, and I would leave for Illing Junior High School a short time later. I was brushing my teeth, standing in front of the bathroom sink. There was a very thin stream of water coming from the faucet. For some reason, I looked down at the sink just in time to see the spigot turn on its own, and the water rushing out of the faucet. Holy crap! What was I supposed to say again? What did the Warrens tell me to say??? I struggled to remember, but then:

> *"In the name of God, leave this house, and leave us alone!"*

As fast as the faucet had turned on, it now turned off. I was so scared that I didn't know whether to shit or wind my watch! But it had stopped. That would be the last episode I, or anyone else in the family would experience in our home.

A short time later, Jessie had graduated from high school, and had moved to Huntsville Alabama, to start her adult life. One night, our house phone rang, and Mom answered it. It was Jessie, and she had one thing to say to Mom:

"Guess who followed me down here."

From what I was told, Jessie sought out another "solution" to the problem, down south. Yet, to this day, more than forty years later, Jessie has never talked about it, and we've never brought it up…

All we know is that Henry is gone.

After-School Jobs

I don't know about you, but I had a lot of different part-time jobs, from the time that I turned sixteen. I would either become easily bored, or it would interfere with something I wanted, or needed, to do.

The very first job I had was at this brand-new type of store, which was opened on the corner of Main and Delmont Streets. It was one of the first of its type in the United States, and certainly the first in Manchester. It was a "convenience" store, called 7-11. What a unique concept! The name meant that it was open from seven in the morning till eleven at night! Get it? Seven… Eleven!

The store was originally owned by Mr. and Mrs. Goolsby. Mr. Goolsby hired me to stock shelves and sweep-up. I got free Slurpees! This was a new drink, guaranteed to give you massive brain freeze. I only worked ten hours a week and wanted more. But there were no additional hours to be had. So, I looked elsewhere.

Then, I got a job at Tacorral, on Broad Street. I was a dishwasher and worked every shift I could get. It wasn't easy work. The kitchen was unbearably hot, from the steam emanating from the dishwasher, and the steam tables, where the meals were made. Remember, this was before microwave ovens. We received no free meals; not even an employee discount. And, the manager was a "dick" about it. In fact, he was a dick about everything.

The new weekly work schedule would be posted on the bulletin board, by the back door, every Wednesday. If you wanted a day off, you either got someone to cover for you, or gave two weeks advanced notice so "Mister Manager" could work it into the schedule. I had tickets to a Wednesday night Doobie Brothers concert, at Dillon Stadium. The show wasn't for a month, but I wanted to leave nothing to chance.

Now, the thing you have to understand is that, in this era of long hair, "partying" and rock concerts, "Mister Manager" was a severe redneck; a conservative, prejudiced task master, who firmly believed that nothing good ever happened at a rock concert, and that it was all pot smoke and depravity (He was right, but nobody would ever admit it…). So, I never told him the reason that I needed the night off. But he found out. Somebody, with whom I worked, flapped their gums to MM, because I flapped my gums to them.

So, fast-forward to the week before the concert. I walked into work, and immediately glanced at the schedule for the following week. MM had me scheduled for the next Wednesday; the night of the Doobie Brothers Concert!!

> *"Excuse me, MM. There's a mistake on the schedule. You have me working next Wednesday, when I asked for the day off a month ago."*

> *"Well, I need you to work."*

118

"I'm sorry, I can't. I've had something planned for over a month, and I can't get out if it."

"Yeah, I know ALL ABOUT your plans! You're on the schedule, so plan on working."

"No way! I did what you asked! I followed your policy, and now you're telling me that I can't go? You have no right to do that!"

"You'll either be here, or you're fired!"
"Screw you! I quit!"

And, I did.

Next stop, Bonanza Steak House, on Middle Turnpike. This didn't last long; only a few months. Nothing monumental to report, other than that I cut my bicep in a piece of broken glass in a trash bag and was taken to the hospital for three stitches. The boss was pissed that I left before my work was done, so he fired me. Big deal.

It was a short time later that word spread throughout the town that the boss was fired for screwing one of the waitresses on the floor of the dining room.

Then, I went to work at Frank's Supermarket, on East Middle Turnpike; not because I had a great desire to work there, I just saw the potential for fun since this was where Teddy Hanson, Karl Smith, and David Corrado all worked. I was a bag boy. Teddy made it quite clear that bag boys were on the lower rung of the evolution ladder, and that I would never amount to anything, if I were not a shelf stocker. This job didn't last long, either. I don't remember why, but I think I quit in order to become an usher at the State Theater, on Main Street.

As I said in "DSG", *"The State Theater was your typical grand, old theater, with a fully-working proscenium stage, used during the old vaudeville era, a free-standing ticket booth, snack bar and balcony."* I loved this place. There was a piano that no one outside of theater staff knew was behind the projection screen. I would get to work early, go backstage, and just play. I actually met

Susie for the first time at a matinee; she was bringing her brother, Sean, to the movies. I remember her handing the tickets to me, and me handing her the stubs. She smiled and thanked me. I wouldn't know her name for a while, but I never forgot her.

After that, I worked for a while at the Shell Car Wash, on Broad Street, I drove a school bus, and did janitorial work at Sears, at the Manchester Parkade. All of these jobs to fill in the time between school trips to Hawaii, vacations, concerts, and NFB gigs. It was about this time that I stopped looking for jobs, and just played with the band. Hell, I was making a lot more than minimum wage, anyway.

New Year's Eve at the State Theater

As I've said, I had worked for a while at the State Theater, on Main Street. I was there toward the end of its existence, when it was meeting stiff competition from the UA Theaters East, in the Parkade on West Middle Turnpike. But I still thought it was grand, and special.

Being one of the "low men on the totem pole", my boss gave me the unfortunate news that I had to work on New Year's Eve; just me, and the projectionist. I knew this was going to be a useless night and tried to talk him into closing. But, no dice! I would be there, selling tickets, taking tickets, running the snack bar, cleaning up, and being bored out of my mind. After all, I had seen both features, and there was a rumor that the rest of the Delmont Street Gang was having a party. Now, there's only so much a bunch of underage teenagers can do at a party, and it was probably going to be nothing but guys, but I didn't want to miss the fun. Oh well!

So, the big evening arrived, and I was dutifully at my post, waiting for the throngs of movie goers to flood this theater we loved, to set new box office records for a major holiday, to fill their hearts with laughter and tears and emotion that only cinema could provide…

Two people showed up! Big Bert Baskerville, and his girlfriend. I said hello and hoped that they'd take one look at the empty theater and decide to skip the movie. Hah! Funny teenage usher! There would be no party for you, tonight! Only death "snap snap snap"! (Please excuse the obtuse reference to one of my favorite lines from "Happy Days").

BOTH MOVIES! THEY STAYED FOR BOTH FREAKIN' MOVIES! I SOLD EXACTLY ONE LARGE BOX OF POPCORN, TWO SODAS, AND A BOX OF THIN MINTS! WHAT A HAUL!

The total revenue for the night? About six bucks! When the last movie was over, and I had closed-up for the night, I decided to walk home. It was cold, and lightly snowing, and Main Street was absolutely desolate. Anyone who was going anywhere was already there, and midnight was quickly approaching. Soon, cheers of "Happy New Year" would ring out, couples would kiss, and Auld Lang Syne would, once again, be sung horribly off-key by a bunch of partied-out revelers. Truth be told, I was enjoying the walk home. It was peaceful, and quiet, and left me alone in my thoughts. For the next mile-and-a-half, I could be as introspective as I wanted.

I finally reached Delmont Street at around 12:15AM and decided to detour over to the Smiths' house. In all likelihood, Karl and Larry were still up, and I didn't feel like going home, yet. I was walking up the driveway, through the darkness, on my way to the back door, when I heard the muttered sound of moaning, emanating from the backyard. Upon investigation, I found Sid Orlowski, lying face down in the snow. I kneeled down and rolled him over onto his back. He was absolutely shitfaced:

> *"Sid! What the hell are you doing?*
> *"Eric, help me! I can't get up!"*

"What did you drink?"

"Uhh, a buncha Maximus Super."

Now, I don't know if you remember, but the rumor was that one Maximus Super had the alcohol content of three cans of regular beer which, of course, was total bullshit. I think that that rumor was propagated by the same morons who told everyone that Boone's Farm was actually wine! They were <u>both</u> inexpensive, and <u>both</u> godawful!

I vigorously rubbed a handful of snow in Sid's face to help revive him a bit, picked him up, and dragged him toward the back porch. I couldn't leave him in the snow; he would have died of exposure. When we reached the porch, there was Ken Hanson, passed out on the picnic table. I leaned Sid against the nearest tree, and told him to stay there, as if he were actually going to walk away. I went over to Ken and shook him awake. He looked up at me through half-closed eyes, and proceeded to puke straight up in the air, showering his face with beer vomit. I picked Ken up by the collar, dragged him out into the snow, and rubbed his face in it, both to wake him up and, hopefully, wipe off the puke.

When he was reasonably clean, I dragged him into the Smith's den, and laid him on the floor. I went back outside, and dragged Sid into the den, as well. Then, I went looking for other casualties.

I found Karl in the bathroom, passed out with his head in the toilet. I shook him awake, and Karl looked up at me, and moaned "Eric, help me!" I stripped him down to his underwear, threw him in the bathtub, and started running the bath water. Karl just uttered "Thank you".

I decided to explore the basement, and found Larry on the couch, upside-down, with his feet propped up against the wall. I asked him if he was okay, and he said he was. I laid him on the couch, and put a blanket over him, and left him to sleep it off.

For the next couple of hours, I tended to my fallen friends, sobering them up, and making sure there would be no further problems. Eventually, when Karl and Larry were safely asleep in their own beds, I walked Sid and Ken to their respective homes, and got them safely inside, out of the elements.

While I walked home, I thought about how fate plays a part in our lives, and what might have happened had I not had to work that night. And, I realized that it was a good thing I had.

We never really talked about that night, after that. I think everyone wanted to forget it.

Book Smart, not Street Smart

You know, one thing which always shocked and amazed me about Manchester was the fact that there were so many families who never ventured outside of the state. I mean I actually know people who have spent their entire lives in Manchester, who have never visited New York City! This is a strange thought to me, as my mom and dad dragged us all over the east coast and beyond, for years. It was second nature to me.

It was 1974. Grand Funk Railroad was playing at the New Haven Coliseum, and I had four tickets in the tenth row! YES!!! "We're an American Band" was on the charts, and I couldn't wait! Susie, of course, would be my date; and, I promised the other two tickets to my friend, Mike Sherman.

Karl Smith had introduced Mike to me. He was one the nicest guys I'd ever met, and the girls loved him. He had a big smile, big heart, and a great sense of humor. So, it was no wonder that he would be going to the concert with "Julie Midler". Julie was gorgeous, sweet, and an honor student – you know, the type of student who was so brilliant that she ruined the "Bell Curve" for everyone else in the class? Straight A's, outgoing and gorgeous! A great girl, for a great guy.

This was a big deal for all of us, as this would be the first time my parents would allow me to take the family car so far away from home, without parental supervision. I would drive the four of us to and from the concert – a round-trip of 120 miles! I was seventeen, Susie was 16, and Mike and Julie were 15. My dad reassured Julie's parents that I was a responsible driver, and that their little girl would be in good hands. The trip was on!

We had a great time! The concert was huge and loud, with pyrotechnics, big projection screens, and thousands of screaming fans in attendance. To this day, one of the best concerts I've ever seen. Mark Farner, Mel Schacher, Don Brewer and Carl Frost blew the doors off the place!

Some two hours later, the concert was over. We were emotionally spent. The crowd was still buzzing as we all left the arena and headed back to our cars. We did it! We were grown up! We had braved the I-91 highway, ventured into the unknown, and were triumphantly on our way back to Manchester, no longer virgins to the life-changing experience of arena rock.

On the drive home, we talked of the experience, and our favorite moments, while WDRC played in the background. The drive soon became a quiet one, as Mike and Julie took to "kanoodling" in the back seat, while Susie cuddled next to me, in the front. As we reached the outskirts of Hartford, with only a short drive to home, I asked *"Anyone hungry?"*

Dumb question, I know. We were teenagers, and it had been several hours since dinner. Of course, everyone was hungry! There was a pizza or burgers out there with our names on them, so I decided to find an open restaurant.

Not knowing anything about dining opportunities in the Hartford area at eleven o'clock at night, I turned off on Capitol Avenue, in Downtown Hartford, and set out to find a "greasy spoon" to satiate our teenaged lust and iron stomachs. After blindly driving around for several minutes and seeing nothing open (This being Hartford in the seventies, the sidewalks traditionally rolled up at 6:00 PM on Saturday…), I happened to turn up Prospect Street in order to head back to Manchester.

We were crawling up the deserted street, between the closed banks and office buildings, when I happened to look over to my right, and saw a familiar sight. There, in all its majestic glory, was the Hartford Times Newspaper Building. Built in 1920, the building boasted six giant marble pillars, as part of its classic façade. It looked like the Parthenon, in Rome. Or, at least I thought so. I had visited there on a field trip during my days at Bentley School, and there it was again.

I exclaimed: *"Hey look! There's the Times Building!"*

From the back seat, in that sweet, demure voice that only Julie could produce, she said matter-of-factly: *Oh, then this must be Times Square!"*

Through the darkness, I glanced over at Susie who, with a look of wide-eyed shock on her face, said nothing. She just silently mouthed the word *"Whoa"*. I looked at Mike through the rearview mirror, and he just gave me a look as if to say *"I've got nothin'."*

In the most-diplomatic demeanor I could muster, I said *"Julie, Times Square is in New York City."*

"Ohhh, that's right!"

We made it back to Manchester, found a diner, and ate over small talk. I drove to Julie's house, and Mike escorted her to her front door. He gave her a kiss goodnight, she went in the house, and turned off the porch light. The date was officially over.

Mike climbed in the back seat, and I started the drive to his house, to drop him off. For what seemed like several seconds, nothing was said; until I heard Mike mutter in a sarcastic tone: *"Times Square???"*

We busted up. It was simply a funny moment in its innocence and naiveté. None of us wanted to embarrass Julie, so none of us ever brought it up, again.

But, if there's a moral to the story, PLEASE expose your kids to something beyond the confines of your hometown. It's a big world out there, with a lot of it only a short distance away.

The Manchester Parkade

How could I not talk about the Parkade??? I loved going down there! Yet, I almost totally ignored it while writing DSG! A pox upon me for being a lout!

As you know, if you grew up in Manchester, the Parkade is in two strip mall sections. The front section, for years, was anchored by Sears. Now, that spot is occupied by Stop-n-Shop. Residents affectionately refer to it as "Stop-n-Talk", because it seems as if you're always bumping into someone you know, and this adds another twenty minutes to your shopping trip; much to the chagrin of your whining kids, who just want to go home.

For as long as I can remember, the Parkade had this God-awful faded-green façade. There were offices on the second floor; but I've never known anyone who worked up there. The back section was anchored by the new location for King's Department Store, which had moved over from Hartford Road location, in the Cheney Mills.

The Parkade was the main competition to the Main Street Stores, right up to, and including, the UA Theaters East, which ended up being the death knell for the State Theater.

The Parkade Bakery was there. I looked forward to going there, with Dad, on the weekends. They had the best butter cookies (with the maraschino cherry on top), fresh-baked rye bread and, my absolute favorites, "Hermit Cookies", which were reputedly made from the leftover batter from other baked good. I adored them – fresh, warm, raisins… Give me a cold glass of milk, and leave me alone! All purchases were placed in salmon-colored boxes, tied with string, which fed from this huge spool, which hung from the ceiling.

Liggett's Rexall Drug Store was there, with its big, orange sign with blue letters. I loved that place! Like its counterpart, Lenox Drug Store, on Center Street, Liggett's was a cornucopia of all things you'd find in a Walgreen's, and then some. There was a soda fountain, huge magazine rack, photo counter, pharmacy and, my favorite part, the tobacco pipe racks. Don't ask me why, but I always loved pipes; the different styles, shapes, and the smell of the burning tobacco. I bought two pipes, there – a Largo straight, and a Dr. Grabow bent. I still have them, to this day, some 45 years later.

W.T. Grants was there! Two floors of anything and everything, including clothes, housewares, furniture, record – you name it. When I was fourteen, my parents asked me what I wanted for my birthday. I told them that I wanted a pine rocking chair that was at Grant's, prominently displayed on the shelf above the stairway which led to the lower level of the store. It came with a green and white scotch-plaid blanket. Fourteen years old, and he wants a rocking chair? Sure! I wanted it for my bedroom. I really had no adult furniture, and this would give Dad somewhere to sit as well, when he came into my room on Monday nights to watch Monday Night Football.

I still have that rocker, AND the blanket, in my Las Vegas home, to this day. Where I go, it goes.

Radio Shack was in the corner of the Parkade. Teddy Hanson worked there for some time. He actually rose to the ranks of manager. That store made him the radio/stereophile he is today. Want to know about sound systems, antennas, or turntables? Ask Teddy.

Bernie's TV and Appliances was in the corner of the front section. This was my dad's go-to store when we needed an appliance, for years; everything from televisions to washer/dryers, to small appliances. The store was rustic, and had a solid customer base, for years.

My favorite store was Reeds Stationers. This place sold the coolest pens! Every school year, I insisted upon buying my school supplies there. To this day, I remember buying an olive-green Paper Mate click pen. If you had a Paper Mate, you were cool. New #2 pencils, erasers, rulers, protractors, paper tablets, and the best book selection in town! I used to buy all of my Conan the Barbarian paperbacks there, along with Tolkein, H.P

Lovecraft, and others. Going here always gave me the 'warm-and-fuzzies". I would go there, while Mom and Dad were shopping elsewhere. It was just a comfortable place.

The Parkade Bowling Lanes were there. League nights, birthday parties, pinball machines, and the snack bar. For years, it was the "go-to" place for first dates, family time, or a cheap form of babysitting, while mom and dad shopped. It's gone, now. And, that's a shame.

Card Gallery was one of the places to buy greeting cards, candles, blacklight posters, band posters, gag gifts, and gifts for any occasion. I used to love the smells emanating from there, from the lamp oils to the candles.

David's Nightclub was one of the great night spots in the Greater Hartford area. All the top local bands of the day played there, including Oreo, Little Village, Vice, P.F. and the Flyers, Circus, Hot Head Slater, and even the Nifty Fifties Band. David Woodbury was the owner, and he made it one of the places you wanted to hang out. I always liked David. He was always approachable and friendly. Once you were a part of the "David's Family", he always made you feel welcome. Here we are, all these years later, and David's has a tribute page on Facebook. To me, that says a lot.

Christmas was always fun, at the Parkade. It was one of two places you did you shopping – that, and Main Street. There was no Buckland Mall, as there is today. These were your local choices, unless you drove out to Caldor's, which was down the hill from where Buckland Mall is, now. Ancient holiday decorations, showing the years of wear, were wrapped around light poles. Carols played over stereo speakers, placed outside by Radio Shack; Sears all decked out for the holidays, causing the anticipation level of little kids to boil over, as they dragged mom and dad through the toy section, with their "desires" circled in the Sears catalog – the best catalog ever created; Holiday cookies at the bakery; and, carolers, appearing intermittently during the days leading up to Santa's visit.

You actually thought I would forget, didn't you? You thought I was going to wrap up this chapter without paying homage to the one constant, the one stalwart survivor which, despite openings and closings, or the decades marching by, each and every one of us can look forward to the time-tested repast of EVERYONE'S FAVORITE RESTAURANT…

(Wait for it…)

Shady Glen! That perfect purveyor of the glorious crispy-cheeseburger, the <u>Bernice Original</u>, the condiments served in the four-square aluminum serving carousels, the shot glass-sized paper cups full of water, with the SG logo, and the names John and Bernice Reig, printed on them. And let's not forget the murals of sugary-sweet elves, eating ice cream and frolicking around…

ICE CREAM! Let's not forget that! SG ice cream is the best!!! And, the special, seasonal flavors; Watermelon, Rum Raisin, Pumpkin, and Egg Nog…

142

There was never a bad time, never a bad meal. Like hot dogs, apple pie and Chevrolet, Shady Glen is American to the core. And, to this day, people come from all over the country, and the world, to experience a Bernice Original. I know I do.

D&L Clothing, Manchester Jewelers, Treasure City, Adam's Apple, Butterfield's (then Marshall's), Savings Bank of Manchester, Hartford National Bank, Connecticut Bank & Trust, and a host of other stores came in and went out over the decades. The players may have changed, but the game was the same.

The Parkade struggles on. It's seen its better days, fighting for its share of the consumer pie, against the Buckland Mall, or a half-dozen other malls around the area, which boast indoor, air-conditioned comfort. It's not new, it's not pretty, but it's still there, with plenty of parking, a bunch of friendly, hard-working people and a lifetime of memories for anyone lucky enough to see it in its heyday.

Do yourself, your kids, and your grandkids a favor; take them by the Parkade. Share your memories. Buy 'em a cheeseburger. Tell 'em about the "Glory Days".

I'll bet your memories are good ones!

One Night in November, 1974

I was sick and tired of being sick and tired. I was done with being afraid to step into my own; afraid that people would laugh at me for following my dream! I wanted to play music, to perform in a band. After all, I had been in several as a drummer; none of them very good. And, I had a vision that I wanted to bring to fruition. I wanted to form an Oldies Rock-n-Roll band, just like my heroes, in Sha Na Na.

I had been a fan of fifties music well before the genre had seen a rebirth because of Grease or Happy Days. It was actually Bill Haley's "Rock Around the Clock", which I had purchased on an oldies compilation album in the seventh grade that fueled my love for all things fifties and doo wop. Then, when American Graffiti came to Manchester's State Theater, I had drunk the proverbial "Kool-Aid", and needed to do something about it!

It was the new school year – 1974. I was a senior. This was supposed to be my <u>best</u> year! But, after years of feeling like I was nothing in the grand scheme of school life, just another faceless kid in the halls, I was ready for a change. The Manchester High School Talent Show, which was another one of Martha White's productions, had been holding auditions for most of the week, and it was the last evening of auditions, being held in the Bailey Auditorium, and judged by a panel of students.

Since I was at the school for Roundtable practice, and this was my last chance, I moved. I made a bee line over to the tenor section and stood in front of Brian Beggs. Brian was a junior, a huge Beach Boys fan, and had a crystal-clear "Brian Wilson" falsetto, and was a heartthrob; the girls loved him!

> *"Brian! Wanna be in the talent show with me? I wanna sing some doo wop!"*
> *"Sure! Who else is gonna do it?"*
> *"Don't know.*

Then, I looked at Jonny Adams.

Jonny and I had known each other since we were little.
Our parents were founding members of the Little Theater
of Manchester, so we were always bumping into each
other, although we attended different elementary
schools, and Jonny was in advanced classes in junior
high and high school, while I would have been riding the
"special bus", if I didn't walk to school.

I saw Jonny as the romantic lead singer. He would be the
one to sing all the teenaged songs of angst and car
wrecks, and breakups. He had a golden voice and, he
too, was a heartthrob.

> "Jonny, wanna be in the talent show? We're
> gonna sing doo wop."
> "Yeah. Sure. Why not?"
> "Okay, who else?"
> "How 'bout Neil Snuffer?"
> "Neil! Wanna be in the talent show with us?
> We're gonna sing doo wop."

"Okay!"

Neil was a twin. He and his brother, Lee, were everyone's friends. Everyone liked them, and they were cool with everyone. Neil was yet another good-looking kid. See, there was a method to my madness; not only did they have talent, but the girls would flock to the shows. And, of course, the guys would follow. So, now we had our singers. Beggsie, Jonny, Squealin' Neil, and me, Rocko. Three heartthrob tenors, and one big, ugly bass.

But we needed accompaniment. There WAS only one choice. No one else would do. It HAD to be Terry Sullivan. Terry was a monster on piano – plain and simple. He was Harry Connick, junior before the ever WAS a Harry Connick, junior. He played a very mean, very soulful piano for an Irish kid from Manchester. I was in awe of his ability.

*"Hey Terry! Wanna be in the talent show? We
need ya to play piano! We're gonna sing doo
wop!"*

"I LOVE doo wop!"

"Let's go!"

That was it. No long decision process; just grab the guys
and learn a song. We went into one of the practice
rooms, and gathered around the piano. We decided to
learn "Come Go with Me" by the Del Vikings. Brian
would sing the lead, and I gave Jonny and Neil their
background parts. A few times through to rehearse, and
we headed to the auditorium, to audition. We sang, and
were told we were in. Just like that.

But we weren't complete. There was something missing.
We needed a Tenor Saxophone player! The following
day, I went to see Mr. Andrew Shreeves, the MHS Band
Teacher. I asked him if he could recommend a sax
player. Without hesitation, he turned toward his class,
and called one of the kids to the front of the room.

"Eric, meet Mitch Dul. He's the one you want."

Mitch was this wide-eyed sophomore, whose whole life revolved around his studies, and his sax. I would find out later that this kid was a frigging genius! I mean savant-like! I told him what we were doing and asked him if he wanted to join us.

Uhhhh, sure. I guess so…"

NOW, all the pieces were in place. Except for one little detail - we didn't have a name, and the programs were being readied for print. It was Martha White who came up to me, and said *"You don't have a name? How about the <u>Nifty Fifty Boys</u>?"*

How cool was that? So, we were set – two songs, greaser wardrobe, a name; we were ready. We would soon find out that the "powers that be" had scheduled us as the last act of the show. Nothing like adding a little MORE pressure!

On Friday November First, 1974, Bailey Auditorium
was jam-packed! The acts were taking the stage one after
the other, while our anticipation, and nerves, festered.
Finally, it was our turn. From the auditorium exit, stage
left, I turned and asked the guys if they were ready. I
took my fist, and pounded on the closed door, and flung
it open, with a CRASH! I led this band of greasers into
the auditorium, with sneers on our faces, and Wildroot
Hair Cream dripping from our heads.

This crowd of parents, teachers and students exploded
into applause and cheers, and jumped to their feet! We
were getting a standing ovation just for entering the
room. After several minutes of clowning, and preening
and milking the audience, we finally settled in front of
our microphones, and I counted off: *"1,2,3,4,5,6 –
1,2,3,4,5,6..."* and, we sang our first song, at our first
performance – "Silhouettes" by the Rays, with Jonny
singing lead. Girls were screaming, adults were beaming,
and they were swaying on their feet. Holy crap! What a

reaction! We followed with "Come Go with Me". The response was equally explosive. We danced, and strutted, and sucked it all in! We did it!

When we finished the act, another "standing – o". We lined up to take the curtain call with the other acts and were met with another volley of thundering applause. None of us realized that our lives had just changed in a very big way. To borrow a line from the 80's movie, Can't Buy Me Love, we "*went from no status, to king status, overnight*". We were no longer nameless faces in the halls of MHS!

From that moment, everyone was my "lifelong friend". Fellow classmates who would never give me the time of day, wanted to hang out with me. It was a difficult task to weed out the fair-weather friends and remember those who had always been there for me. I remember people telling me how great they thought my band was, and I would look at them sideways, waiting for the insult I thought would be coming. But it never did. I had to learn to just say "thank you".

We soon became a legitimate band, adding Mike Armentano (74), Steve Armentano (77), Charlie Uzanas (73) and Bill "Bubba" Matthews (75) – all proud MHS-ers. And, we started playing concerts all over New England, to crowds upwards to several thousand. We've opened for famous national acts, recorded an album, and had more fun than any bunch of guys should be allowed to have. We were now the Nifty Fifties Band.

Nifty Gigging

"We do so many shows in a row,
And these towns all look the same,
We just pass the time in our hotel rooms,
And wander 'round backstage,
Till those lights come up and we hear that
crowd,
And we remember why we came…"

- Lyrics from The Load Out, by
  Jackson Browne

These lyrics are amazingly accurate. Outside of the time onstage, the rest of the time mostly sucks. Traveling, set-up, take-down, late-night diners, catch some sleep, maybe hit the pool at the hotel, then start all over again.

When we started playing clubs, Steve Armentano and Mitch Dul weren't even eighteen, the legal drinking age in Connecticut, at the time. So, we had to make promises to their respective mothers to look out for them and keep them out of trouble.

The first nightclub gig we ever booked was at Club 21, a strip club by day, in East Hartford, near Pratt and Whitney Aircraft, whose workers made this a regular hangout. By night, the management would bring in local bands. I hated this place; so sleazy. The only thing I really remember about the place was that when we started our show, a couple of strippers got up to dance, and were booed-off stage: "Sit down! We wanna watch the show!"

Early on, one of our regular haunts was The Rusty Nail, in Glastonbury. This was a rustic club, on New London Turnpike. Not much to look at, but it had a great crowd. And, since it was so close to Manchester, our fans would show up in droves. The stage was way too small for a band of our size, so the singers had to be on the floor in front of the stage. This, in and of itself, was troublesome, as there was no protection for us from the crowd.

Case in point, one night, the crowd was fairly large, and the dance floor was packed. At one point during the show, there was this hefty-looking biker-type guy dancing directly in front of Jonny. During one particular song, the biker would dance backward toward Jonny's microphone stand, becoming perilously close to the point that Jon would grab the mic stand out of self-defense, fearing that he would be smashed in the mouth with the mic, itself. This went on for several minutes, with Jonny doing a fine job keeping his cool and protecting his teeth...

...Until he took his eyes of the biker for one split second. BLAM! Right in the mouth with the mic! Jonny lost it. With a forward thrust kick straight out of Jon's years of Kung-Fu training, the biker went careening through the crowd, taking four or five people with him. It looked like someone had bowled a strike! Thankfully, Jonny only suffered a split lip; not dental damage.

Our girlfriends would occasionally be in the crowd during our shows. This was a given at "the Nail" as, again, it was so close the Manchester. And, it was understood that the girlfriends were free to dance with someone, if asked; no big deal. One night, this guy asked Susie to hit the dancefloor. She accepted. The band soon transitioned from a fast song to a slow dance. The guy grabbed Susie and they continued to step. That's when the following conversation took place:

> Guy: *"So, do you come here often?"*
> Susie: *"I follow the band."*
> Guy: *"Oh, you're a big fan?"*
> Susie: *"My boyfriend's in the band."*
> Guy (Pointing to Bubba): *"Is he the little one on the end?"*
> Susie (Gesturing toward me): *"No, he's the big one in the middle."*

In mid-song and mid-step, the guy stepped away from Sue, thanked her for the dance, and scurried off leaving her standing alone on the dance floor. Was it something she said?

The Nifty Fifties Band would spend several weeks during the summer playing around the Saybrook,

Connecticut area. Actually, we would rotate between three clubs – The Cavern, The Velvet Touch and the Black Swan Marina. Each had their distinct crowd of regulars, while the crowd would be flushed out with our group of followers, who would show up at each club. When we weren't off performing a "one-nighter" somewhere, we were mostly in and around the Long Island Sound.

Our summer gigs would start immediately after final exams, and continue through Labor Day. It was a great time, but tiring, even for a bunch of teenagers. We had purchased an old school bus,
and had converted it for our band, to travel together and haul our equipment. Charlie would do most of the driving, with Neil relieving him. It was a lot of fun, and beat the hell out of driving five cars full of equipment to a gig. Anyway, exams were already over for Neil, his twin brother Lee, and I. So, we were charged with driving the equipment to the Cavern Lounge,
in Saybrook for our weeklong engagement. which would start the following night. This way, the other guys would

not have to worry about moving equipment on an exam day.

Lee, Neil and I arrived at the Cavern on Thursday evening, and would unload our equipment after that evening's entertainment had concluded. So, we decided to enjoy ourselves at the club.

The Cavern was unique in the fact that its themed décor consisted of plaster stalactites protruding from the ceiling. These stalactites, in and of themselves, would produce their own fun, as people would make friendly wagers on who would jump up too high and impale themselves through the tops of their skulls.

In all modesty, we were treated like VIP's when we were at the Cavern. The owner, Frank, would comp our bar tab, buy us dinner; whatever we needed. We were a money machine for him, and he went out of his way to keep up happy. So, when we had arrived that evening, things were no different. We paid our respects to Frank, and also said hello to the head bouncer, Lou.

Lou was an anomaly, as bouncers go, as he was about Six feet two inches tall, muscular and handsome, and friendly. He was a nice guy, and we enjoyed talking with him. But we knew better than to mess with him, as Lou was also a high black belt in karate. He was truly a good friend to have.

It wasn't long after we had arrived that a table of NFB fans invited us to join them. We obliged, and joined them for an evening of drinks and conversation. And, we were having fun. To set the scene, I was sitting with my back to the stage, facing the front door of the club, with Neil and Lee sitting directly across from me. Lou was sitting on his stool, by the door. Our hosts, a young couple, were sitting to my left, with the young lady sitting between her boyfriend and me.

The evening was progressing nicely when, out of the blue, these two big hands grabbed my face!

My head was involuntarily wrenched around to make
eye contact with this big, fat drunken sack of shit, who
immediately started giving me orders in a menacing
manner:

> *"I don't want you talking to her (referring to our*
> *hostess)! You can talk to him, him, and him, but I*
> *don't want you talking to her!*

The whole time, he's accentuating his point, by forcing
My head around to see each person to whom he has
referred.

I looked at Lee, who's had this look on his face that told
me he's about to jump into the fray. I looked at Lou the
bouncer, to see him removing his glasses.

> *"If you're smart, you'll take your hands off of*
> *me, right now."*
> *"What did you say???"*
> *"You heard me! Remove your hands, and this*
> *goes no further."*

"Mr. Sack" abruptly let go of my face. Thinking the incident was over, I looked up to get a better look at my assailant, when BOOM! The bastard hit me square in the jaw with a sucker punch. I flew off of my chair, onto the floor. I was lying there, trying to clear my head. While all around me I heard screaming, glass breaking, and tables flying. When I finally pulled myself to my feet, I looked down, to see Lou sitting on the back of my assailant, wrenching his head back via a chin lock, in a most-uncomfortable looking position.

Lou asked me what I wanted to do with him. I told Lou to throw him out and call the cops. Lou did just that. But it wasn't over. While escorting "Mr. Sack" out of the club, the moron made a fatal mistake, by taking a swing at Lou. About five seconds, and five punches later, this mental midget was lying in the gravel parking lot, in an unconscious state, looking like a walrus sunbathing himself. The cops showed up, and took him to jail.

And, I played the opening night of the engagement with a fat lip.

We played every kind of gig, in every possible setting. One time, we played a Girl Scout camp in Northern Massachusetts. We had to travel through a driving rainstorm to get there. We were worried about Beggsie, as he was two hours behind us, driving up in his orange VW Super Beetle. As we're chugging along, slowly approaching our destination, we heard this familiar noise; the winding of a VW engine, as Beggsie went flying by. How that maniac ever caught up to us is beyond me!

So, we played the gig in front of two hundred screaming, giddy Girl Scouts, while under the watchful eye of their suspicious chaperones, who were there to ensure that we played music, and nothing else. At the end of the show, we were escorted to our private cabin, where we would bed down for the night; and, absolutely nothing untoward happened, except for the fact that I woke up in time to find the guys trying to dip my hand into warm water, in hopes of making me wet my bed. AND, THEY HAD THE GALL TO BE DISAPPOINTED!

Assholes!

Yeah, practical jokes were a staple of the band.
Everybody took the hit, at one time or another.
One time, during a winter engagement at the Cavern
Lounge, between Christmas and New Year's, I had
thrown a bucket of ice water over the shower curtain, on
top of Beggsie, who immediately vowed revenge. I was
now on my guard.

Two days later, and ever-aware, I was in the same
shower, when I saw the bathroom door slowly
open. I knew I was about to be the victim of the same
fate, and scrunched-up in the corner of my enclosure to
avoid the icy shower. And, here it came; a bucket of
chilled ammo poured over the top of the curtain rod,
missing me completely. In a triumphant, boastful
manner, I flung open the curtain, and yelled out an
obnoxious call of "MISSED ME"…

There, I saw Beggsie, Neil and Steve, armed with two
snowballs apiece. Bang! Zing! Pow!

The perfect ambush! They laid me to waste in the tub, lying there like Janet Leigh, in <u>Psycho</u>, with the welts left by their well-planned attack reminding me that payback is, and always will be, a bitch.

For purposes of this next segment, I will just refer to my bandmate as "Mr. Nifty", in order to hide his true identity. As you may imagine, playing in a band attracts a fair share of female fans. And, many were not too shy about pursuing the boys in the band. During the same winter gig at the Cavern, there was this particular girl who was giving Mr. Nifty the "F-me Eyes" all night.

The show was over, and we were preparing to return to our hotel, when Mr. Nifty tells me that he would be going to breakfast with "Miss Eyes", and he would meet me back at our room, which we shared, later on. So, I headed back to our room, which was a typical hotel room, with two queen-sized beds, separated by a bed table with a lamp, with one long common headboard. I showered, put on my jammies and went to bed. It didn't take much time for me to fall fast asleep.

166

Sometime later, I was awakened by loud knocking. In my stupor, I stumbled to the door and opened it, to find Mr. Nifty and "Eyes" standing there. Without saying much, I just turned around, and flopped back into bed. I glanced over to see Mr. Nifty and Eyes sitting on the edge of his bed, watching television. A short while after that, I woke to find the two of them making out. *"Oh great! Here we go!"* I thought. I rolled over, pulled the covers over my head, and drifted off into a deep, deep sleep... until...

BAM! BAM! BAM! BAM! (What the Fuck is going on?)
BAM! BAM! BAM! BAM! (Why is the headboard slamming into my skull??)
I opened my eyes and, through the darkness, there's Eyes, stark naked, bouncing up and down on Mr. Nifty like she was riding a bull in a rodeo! (Oh, for the love of God! I just want to sleep!)
I pulled the pillow over my ears and, finally, fell asleep for the last time that night.

The following morning, a ray of sunlight squeezed through a gap in the blinds, and shone in my eyes, waking me up. I glanced at my watch; it was a little after eight. I looked over, and Mr. Nifty and Eyes were asleep. I laid there for several minutes, trying to shake the cobwebs, when Mr. Nifty woke up and looked over at me. I flipped him the finger and, with this huge shit-eating grin on his face, he walked into the bathroom, to take a shower. I hated him, right there! I don't do well on little sleep.

While I was coming out of my stupor, "Eyes" woke up, looked over at me, and said *"Good morning!"*, as if the circumstances were all so normal. I uttered *"Uh huh."*

> *"Do you always sleep in pajamas?"*
> *"I do when it's ten degrees outside, and I'm by myself..."*

Just about then, Mr. Nifty walked out of the bathroom,

towel wrapped around his waist, another drying his hair, when "Eyes" looks at me, and sheepishly said "*Okay, I'm going to take a shower, now.*" I replied: "*And...?*"

"Well, turn around!"
"Are you fucking KIDDING ME??? You kept me awake, all night long, jumping up and down on my buddy, and NOW you're shy???

With a huff, "Eyes" wrapped her blanket around her body, and hustled into the bathroom. Mr. Nifty looked at me, giggling. I glared at him, through bloodshot eyes, muttered something about hating his guts, and rolled over to go to sleep.

When I woke, hours later, she was gone, never to be seen again. But she left Mr. Nifty the gift that keeps on giving; a dose of the Clap. A trip to the doctor, and he was fine.

We once played a huge motorcycle rally at the Frank Davis Resort, in Moodus, Connecticut.

And, these guys were there to party. During the course of the afternoon, when the audience was good-and-lubricated, there was this scrawny-looking, hag of a woman dancing alone on the dance floor, who decided to "flash" the audience. She pulled up her shirt to reveal what can only be described as two wrinkled sweat socks, where her breasts should have been. It was truly so disgusting that the boys in the band simultaneously turned their backs to the audience, and continued to sing, facing our drummer, Steve, who was in hysterics by this point. When the song ended, we peeked over our shoulders to see that our "private dancer" had finally, thankfully, covered up. The audience was exploding with laughter!

While I was attempting to introduce our next song, our dancer interrupted:

> *"You think I'm a PIG, don't you??"*

I graciously replied:

> *"Lady, you said that, not me!"*

The audience cheered.

Over the years, we would play gigs large and small, from several dozen in the audience to several thousand. We played the very-first "First Night Hartford", and several more thereafter. We appeared on television and radio, and opened for national acts, including the Five Satins, The Drifters, The Mamas and the Papas, and Johnny Maestro and the Brooklyn Bridge. We played from Maine down to New York, and everywhere in between. It was a blast to perform, and a drag to travel to get there. But, we did it, together.

There are many more "Nifty" stories. Don't believe me? Read on!

The Ride Home

It was around two o'clock in the morning. Neil Snuffer and I were driving home from a nightclub gig, in Springfield, Massachusetts. Now, there are two routes you can take to get back to Manchester, Connecticut; you can take the highway until you reach Manchester, or get off at Route 5 in East Windsor, and take surface streets. We chose Route 5, figuring we would stop for coffee, and not have to deal with any crazies on the highway.

So, we're moving along, and we're somewhere near Railroad Salvage and that banquet facility, which has been there for years, when the traffic immediately slows to a crawl. What the Hell??? It's two in the morning! Is there an accident?

When we finally reach the logjam, the cars in front of us are gingerly passing this one car, which is stopped in the middle of the street. And, the driver is passed out cold,

slumped over the steering wheel! AND, NO ONE IS
STOPPING TO SEE IF HE'S ALIVE! Selfish jerks!
I turned my car into the banquet parking lot, and Neil
and I run over to our lifeless "friend" in the middle of the
road. The guy is just sitting there, car in park, engine
running, out cold. Finding the passenger door unlocked,
Neil climbed in and turned off the car. He shakes the
driver, and he finally wakes up. He's trashed out of his
mind.

I help "Mister Party Animal" out of the car, and I drag
him to the parking lot, leaning him against my car, while
Neil drives our friend's car out of the road, and parks it
in the banquet parking lot.

In the meantime, another concerned citizen had pulled in
behind us, having witnessed this random act of kindness,
on our part. Now, it was time for the big question – what
are we going to do with Drunky John, here? Having
found his wallet, I pulled out his license, and held it up
in front of his blurry eyes: *"Is this your address? Do you
still live here?"*

Through a haze of beer breath strong enough to gag a maggot, he mumbled *"Uhhhhh, yeah!"*

The other "Concerned Citizen" chimed in: *"Hey! He lives right down the street from me, in East Hartford! I can take him home!"* I actually asked to see <u>his</u> license in a lame attempt to ensure that he wouldn't take advantage of this poor sap. So, we turned over the keys to the neighbor, and went on our way.

Further down Route 5, we eventually turned left on Sullivan Avenue, on the second leg of our trip home. We had reached the strip mall, where the notorious X-rated theaters resided. Across the street, at the bend in the road, is a white house, on a rise. On the front lawn of this house was a car which had run up a telephone pole and was perched on its rear tires. Again, we pulled over, hopped out and ran to the car.

In the car, was another drunken slob, with his forehead split open by the impact. His face was covered in blood. I pried the driver's door open, and we pulled him out of the car. He flopped to the ground, seemingly impervious to pain, and unaware that he was bleeding. Shortly thereafter, the wail of sirens could be heard in the distance. That got "Mister Crash" overly excited, and he tried to stand up and climb back into his disabled car, to escape the approaching authorities. But, no matter how many times he tried to stand, he would fall. His leg was broken and protruding through his pant leg. So, we held him down.

The ambulance and police finally arrived, and they carted "Crash" away. We gave a statement to the police, got back in my car, and drove away.

The final leg of the trip – Sullivan Avenue turns into Adams Street in Manchester, then left on Middle Turnpike. At the top of the hill at Adams and the Turnpike, I look ahead of me, down the hill, at the traffic light at the entrance of the Parkade Shopping Center. There I saw something flickering. I brought it to Neil's attention: "Now, what the hell is THAT???"

There, flipped over and engulfed in flames, was a Ford Econoline Van. AGAIN, I pulled the car over; AGAIN, we jumped out of the car; AGAIN, we ran to the rescue. Both of us were crawling on our hands and knees, trying to find the passengers; the heat becoming more and more intense.

All of a sudden, the driver stumbled out from behind the hedges of the house in front of which he had crashed. I asked him if he was alright. He replied, *"I think so."*

I asked him if there was anyone in the van with him. Thankfully, there wasn't. He explained that he was on his way home from work, when a car, apparently leaving David's Nightclub, ran the red light on the way out of the Parkade Shopping Center, cut off the Van, and the driver swerved and lost control. The driver of the offending car never stopped to help.

Soon, Manchester Police, Fire and Ambulance arrived. We gave our witness report and were sent on our way.

Neil and I drove the rest of the way to his house, on Autumn Street, without saying another word. I turned the car into his driveway and put it in park. We sat there, staring at the garage door, saying nothing; trying to make sense of what we had just experienced. After what seemed like a lot longer than the five minutes it probably was, I turned and said "Goodnight, Neil". Of course, he replied "Goodnight, Rocko", got out of the car, shut the door, and walked in the house.

We never talked about that night, after that. Why? Because it was so horrific? Maybe. Or, because no one would believe us? Probably.

After all, it <u>was</u> Friday the Thirteenth.

Goofin' on Mike

As much as everyone, including our parents, would like to believe, we weren't pure as the driven snow. There was, OCCASIONALLY, some recreational usage of herbal stimulants (Yeah, that's right! We all drank lots of tea! Get over it!).

Anyway, the NFB wasn't an exception. Traveling all over New England in our own converted school bus, ala the Partridge Family, left a lot of downtime. And, inevitably, a joint or two would be passed around, prior to the gig. Now, I can only speak for myself, but this was not something I could or wanted to do on a regular basis because, on the few occasions I was buzzed during a gig, I would sometimes find myself forgetting where I was during a song: *"Did I sing that verse, yet...?"*. Truthfully, I never messed it up. But I didn't like worrying about the possibility.

As will happen with a "Band of Brothers" in the same condition, we would look for ways to "goof" on each other, either by making said target laugh uncontrollably, or scare the shit out of the intended victim. And, Mike Armentano was everyone's favorite target. I don't know whether he was any more gullible than the rest of us, or whether his reactions were so good the rest of us couldn't help but rise to the occasion.

We were playing at a club called The Inn Place, which was an old federal colonial house, with a wing built onto it, which housed the nightclub. The dressing rooms were on the second floor of the main house, and were easily accessed by going out the exit, at stage left, and climbing the large staircase which was built on the outside of the house; kind of like a makeshift fire escape. We would play our set, go out the exit, climb the stairs, and change or rest, whatever.

So, we had just arrived for a Friday night gig, and none of us were feeling any pain. We set up the equipment and did our sound check. When that was done, we all headed upstairs to get ready for the show; all except Mike, who had stayed onstage, and was tuning his guitars, taking amp levels, things like that. While we were upstairs, I noticed that Charlie was sitting on the sill of an open window, smoking a cigarette. I happened to have looked out the window and realized that it emptied out on the flat-top roof of the nightclub, and that there was a drop to that roof of about two feet. That's when the "wheels of evil" in my head started turning, and a grin came across my face which would have made the Grinch himself, proud. I was going to goof on Mike, but good!

To set the stage, Charlie remained sitting on the windowsill. When we heard Mike coming up the stairs, Beggsie and I started feigning an argument between ourselves which, of course, Mike would witness. I was yelling at Beggsie; Beggsie was yelling at me, and the volume became louder. Finally, the shoving started. I shoved Beggsie, He shoved me. I shoved him again, and he gave me one final HUGE shove. I careened backwards on my heels, and banged into Charlie, and he proceeded to flip backwards out the open window, screaming as he fell!

Everybody played their parts perfectly, with the right dose of theatrical gasps and horror. Mike lost it. Frozen in his tracks, he started yelling *"WHAT THE FUCK??? WHAT THE FUCK??"*

After a few seconds which, to Mike, probably seemed like an eternity, he bolted to the window, screaming *"CHARRRRRLIE!!!!"*. There, he found Charlie, lying on his back, with a shit-eating grin on his face, pointing and laughing: *"Ahhhh-HAH HAH HAH HAHHHHHHH!"*

We all busted up. Mike just stood there, in his flop sweat, muttering *"You fuckin' assholes! I hate you all!"*

I understand that this gag is what helped pay off Mike's psychiatrist's mortgage. And, he doesn't really hate us; he loves us. Just ask him!

Sailing with Beggsie

In the simplest of terms, Brian Beggs was a wild man. He was that proverbial kid who was never told "Don't do that! You could get hurt!" He was the guy who never wore a jacket in the winter and would run across the high school parking lot through a driving blizzard, and act as if he'd been outside sun-bathing. He was the guy who drove his 1971 Clementine Orange Super Beetle like an Indy Race Car, top speed and turning on a dime. In short, he showed no fear at all.

So, we're playing our first weeklong summer gig at the Cavern Lounge, in Saybrook, Connecticut. And, of course, we would have to find accommodations. Mike and Steve were staying at their family's cottage, so that meant that Mitch, Neil, Charlie, Brian and I would have to figure something out.

That's when Brian came up with his BRILLIANT idea:

"I know! We can sleep on my dad's boat! The harbor's not far from here! And, we won't have to pay for rooms!"

Hmm! It sounded good to the rest of us! So, we agreed. We would all sleep on Beggsie's boat, moored in New London Harbor. We drove to the harbor, parked, and walked down to the dock. There, was the Beggs Family dinghy. As this glorified rowboat would only hold four of us, Beggsie decided to swim alongside, while we made our way to our floating hotel.

While we're on the way, Beggsie went missing. The sky was dark, the water pitch black, and we started to get scared. Geoff Blackwell, one of Beggsie's oldest friends, had joined us on this adventure, and started freaking out. He was screaming into the nothingness at the top of his lungs: *"BRIIIIIIAN! BRIIIIIIAN! BRIIIIIIAN!!!!!"*

When the time seemed ripe, and we had all just about lost our collective minds, Beggsie popped up out of the water, laughing his maniacal ass off! Big joke, asshole! I thought Geoff was going to kill him. Finally, we made our way to the sailboat, climbed onboard and, almost immediately, settled below deck to try to get some sleep. It was after three in the morning, and we were physically and emotionally spent. I, for one, didn't waste any time, and fell asleep.

I didn't know exactly what time it was, but it was light out, when I was awakened by our vessel's pitching, and the ongoing conversation on deck. Curiously, I climbed up to the deck, looked around, and was stunned to find that we were out to sea. And, off in the distance, there was the Statue of Liberty! This lunatic had sailed us to New York!

> *"Brian! What the hell are you doing??? We've got a gig, tonight!"*

> *"Reeeelaaaax! We've got plenty of time! We'll be back on time."*

"What about you? You haven't slept! You'll be exhausted for the show!"

"Naaaahhhh! I'll be fine!"

This was just about the wildest thing I'd experienced at the age of eighteen. This was way out of my comfort zone. But Brian was a master. He knew exactly what he was doing and, as usual, had no fear doing it. He got us back to New London with plenty of time to spare, and we played the gig, without a hitch, that night. The rest of us were exhausted but carried on with the show.

We stayed at a motel, that night.

Rock Concerts

The Seventies… this was an amazing time for rock concerts, in Connecticut! It was before MTV and music videos; bands had to tour to sell albums. Not like today, where bands tour to pay the bills.

You could go to Dillon Stadium, which was an outdoor football field in Hartford, which was more akin to a high school football field than a stadium, to see the Rolling Stones, the Beach Boys, Doobie Brothers, Elvis Presley, Grand Funk Railroad, Yes, the Grateful Dead, Paul McCartney and Wings, and on and on. And, there was also the New Haven Coliseum, Springfield Civic Center, the Hartford Civic Center, and a host of other venues, which hosted bands, big and small.

Jim Koplik and Shelley Finkel were the big promoters. They were responsible for bringing these shows to town. This was also the era when Ticketron was unveiled – no more driving all over the state to wait in line for the box office to open at the venue which would host the concert;

you could go to Harvest Beads and Silver, owned by Jerry and Karen Satriano. This was THE place to buy concert tickets. The lines would be down the block when tickets for your favorite band went on sale. And, most of the concerts were festival seating! This meant a mad dash when the venue doors opened. But it was tremendous fun running for the best seats.

There was Shaboo, a converted factory in Willimantic, Connecticut, which hosted many amazing acts, including Aerosmith, Journey, Joe Cocker, Lou Reed, Blood, Sweat & Tears, David Crosby, Aztec Two-Step, Tower of Power, and Todd Rundgren. I'm proud to say that the Nifty Fifties Band played there, as well.

There were also smaller clubs throughout Connecticut which became the staple of our lives, every weekend. David's at the Manchester Parkade, was tremendously popular for an "east-of-the-river" club. Toad's Place in New Haven, The Inn Place in Simsbury, Beverly's in Winsted, The Rocking Horse in Hartford, The Other Horse in Manchester, and another twenty or thirty clubs dotted the Connecticut landscape at the time. And, every one of them had live music!

The featured bands became big news in the local market; the more-successful ones would have their respective followers who would travel to each town to see their local heroes. The fans would become friends of the band, as the band members were fairly approachable. The Nifty Fifties Band was no different. We would see the same faces show up time and time again, as we traveled around the New England club circuit. It was a great time.

Circus, Tirebiter, Savage Brothers, Oreo, Little Village, Fountainhead, Eight to the Bar, N.R.B.Q, The Scratch Band, Too Much Too Soon, Swan, Max Creek, and many others, made their way to these clubs, and were responsible for many great memories. These were the bands I would make an effort to see, when I wasn't playing, myself. And, it seemed that there was always a connection between band members. I mean, everyone didn't know everyone else personally, but we certainly knew OF each other, and had a shared respect.

Most of these clubs are long gone; so are the bands.
Some bands still play, in some form; Eight to the Bar,
Savage Brothers, Tirebiter, and N.R.B.Q., to name a few.
The local seventies musicians still play in jam bands,
with memories of the "good old days" when we were all
teenaged/twenty-something rock gods, with visions of
hitting the big time.

But, regardless of each band's level of success, I know
it's a great feeling for them to know that they left a
lasting impression on a whole generation of music lovers
and party animals. And, I'm sure that none of them
would trade those memories for anything in this world.

I know I wouldn't.

Ryan and the Big Lie

As I described in my first book, Ryan Haley was a scam artist, bordering on the sociopathic. I mean, there was rarely a logical reason for his actions. If he thought he could get away with something, the "little voices" took over, and he would do it. Again, if there was a wrong way, Ryan would find it; thus, the nickname, "Wrong Way Haley".

It was 1976. It was summer vacation, and I was "on the road" with NFB, barely seeing my own bed for two months, as we were rotating time between three clubs along the Connecticut Shoreline. Our backyard neighbors, the Holders, were on vacation, as well. They spent summers in their lakefront property and didn't return home until after Labor Day.

I walked in the house around dinner time, and Mom was standing in the kitchen, with a concerned look on her face.

"Eric, do you know anything about some vandalism at the Holders' house?"

"Huh? What are you talking about?"

"Mrs. Holder called. They would like to see you, at their house, at seven o'clock."

"Why me?"

"They said you vandalized their sun porch screens."

"What??? Oh, come on! You KNOW I wouldn't do that, and I wasn't even here!"

Mom reserved comment, which pissed me off. Why didn't she agree that this was something I would never do? Dad just looked at me, out of the corner of his eye, like he was annoyed that my name would even be brought up in a conversation such as this!

The Holders' residence had a huge screened-in porch, which was connected to the back of the house. There were entrances from the driveway, and from the backyard. They had furnished the porch with wing-backed wicker chairs, a picnic table, and various other adornments. For all intents and purposes, it was an outdoor living room. As Dad had a meeting, Mom joined me for the walk around the corner to the Holder homestead. We knocked on the front door, and there, in the living room, was Mr. and Mrs. Holder, and Mrs. Haley and Ryan. There was heavy tension in the air. Mr. Holder started to speak:

> *"Eric, do you know why we called you here, this evening?"*
> *"Not really."*
> *"We wanted to talk to you about the holes poked through the screens on our porch."*
> *"What holes?"*
> *"<u>Someone</u> entered our porch, while we were gone, and was using it as their clubhouse. We found cigarette butts, beer cans, and someone had poked many holes through our screens. Do you have something to say about this?"*

The picture was becoming clearer. I was a suspect.

"Are you trying to say that I had something to do with this???"

Indignantly, Mr. Holder turned toward the Haleys:

"Ryan, would please you repeat what you told me, earlier?"

All eyes were on Ryan. He stood there as he always did, slack-jawed, breathing through his mouth, with an innocent look on his face, as if every word he was about to utter was the word of God:

"ERIC DID IT!"

Did you ever see one of those old Warner Brothers cartoons, when someone blows their top, and the top of their skull pops off, and rattles around, and steam shoots out their ears?

WHAT??? You rotten, lying no good son of a…"
"Eric! Stop!"

"Ma, he's lying! I wasn't even here! I was in Saybrook the whole summer! You know that!"

"You know, Eric has barely been home, all summer."

"He did it, when he was home!"

"Mrs. Haley, you <u>know</u> Ryan's lying…"

But, Mrs. Haley just stood there, with a look of exasperation on her face, as if she had been down this road with Ryan one too many times. Then, Mr. Holder turned to me. And, with a deeply admonishing tone, said:

"Well, Eric, I expect you to make restitution for the damage!"

"Bullshit! I'm not paying one DIME for this! I wasn't here, and you have nothing to prove that I was! Brian did this, and everyone KNOWS it! This has his name all over it!"

"Eric, calm down!"

"No, Ma! I <u>won't</u> calm down! And, if you pay these people for this, I will never forgive you! I did not do this! You want your money?? Take me to court! I'm not paying for something I didn't do!"

And, while I was on a roll, I lit into Ryan:

"Don't let me catch you outside your house! You're a lying, no-good rotten scumbag, and I'll beat the hell out of you, if you show your face!"

And, with that, I marched out of the house, and walked home, with Mom following, close behind.

It would be several days before I would have my chance to exact my revenge on Ryan. But I found him behind Bentley School, cowering behind the concrete stairs, leading to the fifth and sixth-grade classrooms. I felt the rage building inside of me! My fists clenched so hard that I felt like I could crush walnuts! My blood pressure rose! I was prepared to kick the living crap out of him! And, I growled:

> *"Before we do this, I just wanna know! Why? Why did you blame me, when you KNEW that you did it, yourself???"*

Then, Ryan, as only he can do, with that warped logic that only HE considered logical, explained:

> *"Well, you never get into trouble, and I figured one time wouldn't hurt!"*

I <u>swear</u> to you! That's <u>exactly</u> what he said! I just stood there, in awe. Not only did he say it, he BELIEVED it! I was utterly speechless. The anger seemed to drift away, as I stammered while trying to say something meaningful. But I could muster nothing. How could I pound the life out of him? There was something inherently unfair about beating up a kid who was THIS frigging stupid!

I just turned and walked away.

Things We Never Discussed

Face it; if you're a Baby Boomer, you were raised in a much-more innocent time. You parents never discussed problems with you – job layoffs, money problems, alcoholism, spousal abuse, mental illness, infidelity, and a myriad of other sensitive topics. Unless the "discussion" of any of these topics became loud or physical, the kids were kept in the dark. AND, God forbid, the kids DID experience these problems first-hand, they were admonished to never discuss any of these problems outside of the home. SWEEP IT UNDER THE RUG! Act as if things are normal! We must keep up appearances!

Thankfully, despite the occasional "screaming match" between Mom and Dad, we weren't exposed to a lot of problems. But, one time, when I overheard my parents discussing my dad's recent layoff, it freaked me out. I remember asking if we were going to be homeless. Dad assured me that nothing could be farther from the truth, but it scared the crap out of me, nonetheless. That's when I realized that Dad wasn't as "bullet-proof" as I thought he was. He was human, too; not everything he touched turned to gold.

Dad did go back to work very quickly. It was a huge relief. Dad explained to me that, as an engineer, once the project was completed, there was always the chance of a layoff. Fortunately, Dad had a pretty solid career, and was in demand.

I promised myself that I would never do that to my son. I would make sure that he knew that I was human, and prone to mistakes. It's unsettling to a kid to find out that not all is right in your parents' world. And, when some issue raises its ugly head, it's a shock to one's well-being. It's also terribly difficult to live up to dad's image, when he appears to be infallible. It's a lot of pressure. Live and learn.

But I guess that's the way life was. We were insulated. We were much more innocent and unworldly than the kids today. I mean, when I was at Manchester High

School, I never thought in the terms of someone being gay. It truly never entered my mind. And, now that I look back, and think about the people I knew at MHS, who have since "come out", I find myself thinking *"Well, I guess that makes sense."*

When I started thinking about writing this book, I actually reached out to some of my MHS friends who are gay, to get their perspective on what it was like to be gay in the seventies, in Connecticut, at Manchester High School. And, almost to a person, the reply was the same: *"I really didn't know I was gay until after high school!"*

I was amazed! But that was basically the stock answer. Did any of them feel different? Sure. But THEY didn't equate "Gay", either. They were just trying to fit in like any other kid. While I'm sure there had to be those who knew they were gay, it wasn't the norm at that time, in that town. So, even if they DID know in high school, I'm sure they were less prone to come out. It just wasn't done. These were some of the funniest, kindest, smartest, most-talented people I knew at MHS. That's what I loved about them then; that's what I love about them now.

Judge people for their heart, not because they're different.

Unexpected pregnancy was another exception to the rule; unlike today, where popping-out babies seems like a fad. While there may have been more than one girl who ended up pregnant at MHS, there was only one that I ever heard about which had made the gossip mainstream; a popular cheerleader, and her jock boyfriend. There were all kinds of rumors about how "He" wanted to raise the kid, while "She" insisted upon putting it up for adoption. All we really knew is that "She" disappeared for a few weeks, only to return to MHS, sans baby. Again, there was never any discussion, after that.

Mental Illness – How I wish there were more advancements regarding depression, anxiety and the like, back then. I can think of several people – family and friends – who would have benefitted greatly, had they had access to today's remedies. But, again, it was not discussed. There was a stigma attached to seeking professional help; it was truly a taboo subject, meant to be closeted away, lest your family's idyllic image be destroyed in the eyes of your neighbors! What total bullshit!

We had a close friend, who I'll call "Jay" who actually suffered a major nervous breakdown, and ended up in the psychiatric hospital in Norwich, Connecticut, which was lovingly referred to as "The Nut House". There were rumors that his episode was brought on by drugs, but that was never proven to be fact. As far as we knew, he just flipped out one night.

We all drove down to visit our friend, on a few occasions. I remember walking into the Day Room to meet Jay. It was truly like the day room in <u>One Flew Over the Cuckoo's Nest</u>, with several patients off in their respective worlds. Jay was sitting in a chair, baseball cap pulled low across his forehead, mirrored aviator sunglasses, and wearing hospital garb. He was out of it; he barely knew we were there. The whole situation scared the hell out of me. If this could happen to Jay, who was to say it couldn't happen to the rest of us??

Although I haven't seen Jay in years, I do know that he did get well and, as far as I know has lived a normal, productive life.

Suicide was another topic that wasn't in the mainstream. Today, it seems as if there isn't a day that goes by that you don't hear about a teenager trying to take his/her own life. Not in Manchester; until it happened to one of our own.

Steve was a great kid. I liked him; Sue liked him. Hell, as far as I knew, everyone liked him. So, what must have gone on in this seemingly normal MHS student to make him drive to a secluded street, run a hose from his car's exhaust pipe, and into the passenger compartment of the car? Was it something in his home life? Was he suffering from depression? We'd never know. It was never discussed. There was no such thing as grief counseling, back then. The school system didn't send counselors into the classrooms to discuss what had happened; life just went on.

Susie had gone to Steve's funeral. She was heartbroken. When the services were over, she dutifully returned to her classes at MHS. She walked into "Mr. Malkin's" class and sat down. Mr. Malkin told her that she needed a note to return. Sue told him that she was at Steve's funeral. With no emotion, no sympathy, kind words, Mr. Malkin repeated: *"You need a note to return to class."* Sue left the room.

Why did he have to die? Was there nothing that could be done? Did no one see the warning signs? I'm sorry, but that's truly messed up! His friends were devastated by his loss. Again, there was no outlet other than the funeral, and the strength of those sharing their mutual grief. To this day, Steve's death haunts some of his closest friends. His was a life of pain; a life lost way,

way too early, with nothing for his family and friends to do but pick up the pieces and move on.

Whether it's divorce, cancer, abuse, addiction, loss of a loved one, or whatever else, we ALL have had something which has monumentally changed the way we act, think, sleep, trust...

In Catholicism, we are told about Purgatory - the weigh station before Heaven. If Purgatory truly exists, I believe we, on Earth, are living it. THIS is our Purgatory. How we handle this life is the weigh station.

In the end, it's not about how much stuff we own, how much money we make, how self-important we are. It's about how much we love, and how much we're loved by others.

Be there for each other.
Kindness costs nothing.
Let this be your wakeup call.

Departures and Reunions

Mitchell "Youngster" Dul graduated from Manchester High School in 1977. And, we knew his days were numbered. He was preparing to leave for college, and we hated to see him go. But he was destined for great things, as he would eventually go to medical school and become a well-respected opthamologist, and a professor of the Glaucoma Institute of the State University of New York. But I digress…

At the end of his last show with the Nifty Fifties Band, Mitch cried, I cried…

We all cried. Mitch was a brother; IS a brother. He is one of a few people who know what it was like to laugh, cry, sing, play and fight with, and alongside, the other members of the Nifty Fifties Band.

We needed a new sax player and decided to hold open auditions. We placed an ad in the Penny Saver, our local free paper, where everyone advertised things for sale, and bands looked for new members.

After a few unimpressive auditions, this guy shows up at my house, wearing a tee-shirt, shorts, a Panama hat, and a beard that made him look like a demented member of the Amish. His name was Paul Nigro. Never heard of him!

We introduced ourselves to our visitor, and he pulled his tenor sax out of his case and prepared for his audition. When we asked him what songs he wanted to play, he replied "Whatever you want". Oh REALLY? Mister Big Shot's just going to wing it??? Here we are, this well-oiled, well-practiced "professional" band, and he thinks he can keep up??? HAH! I scoff at you!

So, we counted off, and started to play "Shake, Rattle and Roll", the song made popular by Bill Haley and the Comets. Paul exploded into the song, as if he had been playing it every night for years! He played with dexterity, fierceness, and could hit high notes that only dogs could hear! In short, he was amazing!

We played a handful of other songs, and Paulie fit right in, Without a doubt we had a "keeper", and told him so, immediately. There was no need to audition anyone else.

Paulie, as we would come to call him, came from a very-musical family from Windsor, Connecticut. His brothers all played in bands throughout New England. And, Paul's pedigree put him at the top of the Nigro Family heap. He had played with N.R.B.Q's Whole Wheat Horns, Street Temperature, Eight to the Bar, Shaboo All-Stars, and several others. But now, we had him! And, we just raised our musicianship to a whole new level.

The best thing we learned about Paulie was that not only was he a great guy, he was, hands down, the funniest guy we'd ever met! As funny as the rest of us might have been, Paul was hysterical, and would prove that many times over the next few years.

Case-in-point, as you might imagine, when you have a group of teenaged guys, and several are A-type personalities, arguments and power struggles may erupt.

One particular practice, in my parents' basement, Steve Armentano and I got into a heated argument about something, and we were jawing at each other, pretty well. All of a sudden, Paulie decides to interrupt:

>*"Steve…"*
>
>*"Not now, Paul! And, another thing…!"*
>
>*"Steve!"*
>
>*"Not now, Paul! You can take your mic stand, and shove it…"*
>
>*"STEVE!!!"*
>
>*"FOR CRISSAKES PAUL, WHAT DO YOU WANT???"*
>
>*"Is there something up my nose?"*

We all broke up! That was the end of the argument. But that was Paul. He just made us laugh.

One of my favorite "Paulie Stories" was the one he would tell about his brother Pat's birthday present. Pat was gifted a brand-new BB gun, and he and Paul decided to go out to the pond behind their house to shoot it.

214

While they were out there, Pat came across a huge bullfrog, sitting on a rock. And, for whatever warped reason, he decided to make the frog his target. He took careful aim, and fired, just as the frog leapt off the rock, and into the pond. The BB ricocheted. Paul immediately screamed, clutched his face, and howled "*MY EYE! MY EYE!*"

Pat freaked! He started screaming! Out of sheer terror and remorse, he took his birthday present, and repeatedly bashed it against the rock, shattering it into several pieces. Stunned, Paulie slowly lowered his hands from his face, revealing no injury at all and, with total incredulity, said "*What the HELL did you do THAT for???*

I'm truly surprised that Pat didn't kill him.

We would eventually lose Paulie forever, in the early nineties. He was taken way too soon. There are hundreds, if not thousands, of fellow musicians and fans who have memories of his screaming sax, his humor, and his friendship. I still think about him, and the brothers of NFB reminisce about him, whenever we're together.

As I had explained earlier, we used to play along Long Island sound, quite a bit. During the summer of 1978, we were playing at the Black Swan Marina, in Old Saybrook. I loved this club. The stage was large and elevated. The back wall of the stage was a floor-to-ceiling picture window. Outside that window were several high-priced yachts, moored at the dock. One particular yacht, with a clear view of the stage, belonged to a guy named Francis Albert Sinatra. There were times when I would turn toward the window, and see a shadowy figure sitting on a chair, on the bow of the yacht; the glowing ash of a cigarette moving to the music. One night, at the end of the show, I turned to see this man giving us a standing ovation. I tapped my heart, and pointed to the man, who returned a thumbs-up. He never came into the club; probably didn't want the attention. But I'd like to think he was a fan.

Our week was winding down at the Marina, and the club owner (I'll call him "Tom") called me into his office. When I entered, I noticed that the walls were adorned by many framed photos of Tom, posing with several celebrities. He pointed at one particular photo, and asked: *"Do you know who that is?"*

"Of Course! That's Barry Manilow."

"Well, here's something you probably don't know. I produced his first New England tour."

"Really? How cool is that? Wow!"

"Well, he's getting ready to do another tour. How would you guys like to be his opening act?"

"Say that again...!"

"I said..."

"Yes, please!"

I was over-the-moon excited! I couldn't wait to share this with the band! This was our opportunity! A six-month tour with Barry Manilow!! This would mean a national audience! If we were ever going to hit it big, this was our chance! Feigning my most business-like demeanor, I told Tom that I would discuss it with the rest of the band, and we would get back to him.

I ran back to the guys, who were busy packing the equipment, and told them about this golden opportunity. I was stunned by the mixed emotions. While Paulie, Jon and Neil were excited, Brian, Mike, Steve and Charlie were reticent. HUH??? What was I missing? Why weren't they jumping for joy? It was decided that we would all meet in a few days to discuss this, in detail. I drove home from the gig in a daze, totally confused by the lack of unanimous joy. Again, what was I missing?

A few days passed, and it was time for our meeting. When we were all assembled in my parents' basement, there was noticeable tension on the faces of Mike and Steve. I reviewed the offer with the guys, again. Finally, Steve spoke: *"I can't go."* I was stunned. *"What do you mean you can't go??"*

Steve was the youngest member of the band, and a freshman at UCONN. *"My mom says that if I leave school she'll kick me out of the house!"*

I was incredulous! *"You're only going to be gone for a semester! Doesn't she realize what a great opportunity this is??*

"It doesn't matter. I can't do it."

I could feel my blood pressure rising. Was I actually hearing this?? Did Steve understand the implications here? Did he realize that we would never, EVER get this opportunity again?? I vainly tried to change his mind. It made no difference.

Then, I said something that, at the time, made perfect sense, but I hated saying it: *"Then, we'll have to replace you."*

His brother, Mike, jumped into the fray: *"I'm not playing without Steve!"*

"Then, we'll have to replace you, too! We can't give up this chance! It's not fair to the rest of us!"

This, of course, started a heated discussion, with Brian and Jon taking Mike and Steve's side, while Neil sided with me. Paulie and Charlie seemed non-committal. When all was said and done, I resigned myself to the fact that we had gone as far as we were ever going to go, as sad as that seemed. We would never graduate beyond the local club circuit.

It was then that I made a decision: *"Then, I'm leaving the band. I don't want to only play bars; I want more. And, if you guys are going to pass this up, we're never going to have anything else. I'll leave in January, after the holidays."*

Now, everyone was pissed. It was obvious that I had become Public Enemy Number One.

It would not be too long in the future, that I was informed that Mike, Steve, Charlie, Brian and Jon announced that they were breaking away to start a new band; and, there was no room for Neil and me. They told us that it would be a new concept, not involving the "Nifty Fifties" concept. They offered to buy us out of our share of the sound system, the bus, everything. It hurt. I wouldn't get to say goodbye in my own way; I was essentially being fired from the band that I had started. But I had already started to put my plan into motion; I was going to move the California, and become the "Great American Ac-tor"! But, that's another story.

Contrary to their plan, the guys started playing again as "The Nifty Fifties Band". It didn't last very long, and the band broke up, in 1978.

I would spend ten years in California, toiling away for my "big break". While I had a lot of opportunities, and made a good supplemental acting income, it was never enough to sustain a full-time career. Eventually, Sue and I got married, brought our son home, and bought a house. My "day job" was becoming more lucrative, and I was building a career. Jonny Adams would also move to California for a short stint, and we got back together. We even performed for a while in the same improvisational comedy group. Jonny would eventually move back to Manchester.

In January of 1988, Susie and I had had enough of California, having just survived the Richard Ramirez "Night Stalker" Murders, which terrorized all of Los Angeles, as well as the most-recent Whittier earthquake, which rocked our world to its core. We decided to move back to Connecticut, to have our son grow up with his family around him.

It was June 25, 1988. Jonny Adams was getting married, and Sue and I were invited to the ceremony. When it was time for the reception, we found that we had been seated at the same table as Mike, Steve, Brian and Charlie. And, it was obvious that we were all nervous to be forced upon each other, not having seen each other in years. Thanks, Jonny! You calculating bastard!

But, an hour or so, and several drinks later, we had all loosened up, and joked and laughed and, more-importantly, reminisced about the old NFB days. We were having a great time being together. We were no longer a bunch of headstrong, stubborn teenaged boys; we were adults. There was no animosity, no hard feelings, just fun.

When the reception was over, and we would all be heading back to Manchester, I invited the guys over to our house, to keep the party going. Mike, Steve and Charlie accepted. Brian had to head home and had a long drive.

So, we went home. It ended up with the wives "coffee-klatching" upstairs, while the "boys" were in the basement, joking around. That's when I walked up to Mike and said *"Mike! Let's do it, again!"*

"Do what?"

"Let's put the band back together!"

You could have heard a pin drop. Hesitantly, Mike said:

"Oh, I don't know..."

But I continued: *"Mike, can you honestly say that anything you have done was ever as good as the times we had with NFB? Think about it. We're older; the old bullshit means nothing anymore! We have an opportunity to do it all again, but better! What do the rest of you guys think?*

After several minutes of conversation, it was decided. The Nifty Fifties Band would be re-born!

It's more than forty-five years later and, despite one short hiatus the NFB was still going strong until 2018, with Jonny Adams, Mike and Steve Armentano, and Marty Moran keeping the flame burning. I mean, think about it; this started as a last-minute talent show audition, and has endured, despite all of the years, and personnel changes. And, for that, I'm tremendously proud.

The band finally called it quits a short time ago. When our long-time manager, Cheryl Scott passed away, that was, essentially, the death knell.

Although some of us have moved away, me included, I try to stay in touch with all of them. Whenever I returned to Manchester, I would try to sit in with the band. And, it was like riding a bike.

I still think of all of the members of NFB as my brothers. In honor of them, here's a roster of everyone who "wore the grease" with the NFB:

Brian "Beggsie" Beggs – Vocals

Jonny "Vaselino" Adams – Vocals and keyboards

"Squealin'" Neil Snuffer – Vocals

Bill "Bubba" Matthews - Vocals

Mitch "Youngster" Dul – Tenor Sax and Vocals

Terry "The Tiger" Sullivan – Piano (RIP)

Charlie "Bones" Uzanas – Bass guitar and vocals

Paul Silver – Piano

Paulie "Stuffins" Nigro – Tenor Sax (RIP)

Mike "The Spike" Armentano – Lead guitar and vocals

Steve "Greased Lightnin'" Armentano – Drums

Marty "Bugs" Moran – Bass guitar and vocals

Eric "Rocko" Mann – Vocals and Percussion

I'm honored to know them, and to have shared this experience together. There are 13 of us who know what it was like to be a part of the "Nifty" experience. And, I'm glad to have shared it with all of them.

After all, Rock-n-Roll <u>is</u> here to stay.

Mother and Son Talk

It was 1978. I was ready for a change, and decided I was going to move to Hollywood, California, to become the GREAT AMERICAN AC-TOR!!! I loved performing, loved the stage, and knew I had to move to where the "business" was, if I was going to have a chance. So, I gave my parents the news.

They were both supportive. I knew that, probably, in the back of their minds, they figured that I would go, and get it out of my system. So, I made my plans. I would take a bus to Chicago to visit my Uncle Bernie for a week then fly to Los Angeles, where Johnny Graff would meet me. I would stay with him, in his apartment, until I got my own place. I had a thousand dollars saved, and this seemed as good a time as any. Move date: November first; four years to the day after the debut of NFB. Kind of ironic, huh?

So, here it was, the day before I officially moved out of my parents' home. I was finishing my packing, when

Mom called to me, and asked me to come down to the living room. So, I dutifully obliged. I sat on the love seat, directly across from Mom, and she had a concerned look on her face.

"Sit down; I want to talk to you".

"Ohhh-kay. What's up?"

"Have you ever used drugs?"

"What kinda question is that, just before I leave?"

"I'm just worried, that's all."

"Ma, have you ever seen me wasted, other than that one time I came home drunk?"

Well, no... I can't tell."

"Well, alright then."

"You didn't answer the question."

"What question?"

"You <u>know</u> what question! So, answer me!"

"I've smoked pot,"

"Ohhh Eric!!!"

"Ma, it's no big deal. I've never spent one dime on the stuff and have only smoked occasionally."

230

"Then, how do you get it?"

"You know, at a party or something like that, and the bong gets passed around…"

"What's a bong?"

"It's a big water pipe. They come in many colors and shapes. Remember? We used to see them in those shops in Provincetown."

"Which shop?"

"Remember the time we were on vacation with the Haleys, and Matt picked up a vibrator off the counter, and turned it on? And, when he asked the clerk what it was used for, the clerk told him that it was used to make your nostrils bigger? THAT shop."

"Oh, those! I always wondered how those were used."

"How <u>what</u> was used?"

"The bongs…"

"Oh! For a minute there, I thought you were talking about…"

"Shut up!"

"Heh heh!"

"I just worry about you using worse drugs."

"Ma, I have been offered everything, and I mean EVERYTHING over the years, and have <u>never</u> tried any of it. It scares the hell outta me."

"Seriously...?"

"I have no reason to lie to you. I'm leaving tomorrow. What would you do? Send me to my room? Relax. I'm being totally honest!"

"We used to have Marijuana growing wild along the train tracks, when I was a kid in Kansas City, but we never smoked it. It was just there."

"Different times, Ma."

"So, when you smoked it, did you get high?"

"Yeah, Sure!"

"Uhhh, what's it like?"

"Wanna try it? I can go get some, and we can get ripped!"

"OH ERIC! NO! I couldn't do that!"

"Oh, come on! It'll be fun! I'll bet you'll love it!"

"No! Stop it!"

"Ma! Where are you going?"

"You're being stupid! I've got things to do!"

"Come on, Ma! (Needling)"

"Eric! <u>Enough!</u>"

"I love you!"

"Oh, shut up!"

Epilogue

I loved the years of my youth in Manchester. Despite the pains of growing up, I look back on the good times, and they truly outweigh the bad. Although, like probably every other human on the face of this earth, I still cringe at some of the stupid decisions I had made way back when; which is ridiculous, when you think about it.

When we were kids in Manchester, with all the horror stories in the news today about gangs, drugs and violence, we all truly lived an idyllic lifestyle. We were protected as we could possibly be; we were free to roam anywhere we wanted without the thought of pending danger; we were able to experience life and grow up. While there was some heartbreak, I know I wouldn't trade that existence, that childhood, that neighborhood, that town, that high school, those friends, that band, that girlfriend, or those experiences for anything in the world.

For all of this, I consider myself to be a very rich man.

BONUS STORY #1

"My Mom Can Beat Up Your Priest!"

In the Sixties, it was proper decorum to take the kids to church every Sunday. Mom, Dad and the kids would dress up in their finest Sunday clothes, and join the rest of the community at the house of worship or their choice. For the Manns, it was St. Bridget's Church, on Main Street. At least it was for Mom, my sisters and I, as we kids were all baptized Catholic, which was Mom's religion. Not Dad! He had a "Get Out of Church Free" pass because he was a lapsed Jew and got to stay home on Sundays. I was so jealous.

So, there we were, every Sunday, mumbling the lyrics to the hymns, barely opening our lips like all good Catholics, trying not to fall asleep during the sermon, and lining up to receive our weekly wafer from the priest, which signified that our "Do-Over" was complete, and we were free to go out and rack up new sins, for which we would be forgiven the following week. Oh yeah, and you had better not eat meat on Friday, or you were doomed!

Anyway, the "Head Priest" during this time was Father Delaney, a cranky, sullen, mean son-of-a-bitch (And, that's the nicest way to describe him...), who struck fear in kids and parents, alike. I mean, God forbid you would get caught fooling around. You'd probably end up with your photo on a milk carton!

So, here we were, in the midst of the latest "Fire and Brimstone" speech from Father Delaney, when he stopped the sermon short, and walked off of the altar, and started down the main aisle of the church, surveying his "flock". That's when he did something that, to this day that anyone who attended this service, found utterly shocking.

> *"Bob Smith! I saw you pull into the parking lot in your new car! You can afford to put more money in the collection basket!"*

"Fred Jones, I just read in the paper that you were recently promoted at your job! You can afford to put more in the collection basket!"

And, on he went, amidst the gasps and groans of the congregation. At the time, I was too young to understand the tenor of the situation. But boy, were people embarrassed, cowering, and shamed.

Mom had just one emotion. She was PISSED! Without another word, she scooped up the three of us, and marched us down the aisle of the church, and out the doors, while the murmuring grew among the faithful. On the way home, I remember Mom muttering under her breath things like "Who the Hell does he think he is?" and "How DARE he???"

A couple of hours had passed, and I had all but forgotten what had transpired, when there was a knock at the front door. Mom went to answer it. And there, on our porch, was Father Delaney. He immediately thrust open the screen door, and put one foot on the threshold like a determined door-to-door salesman, and wagged his bony finger in Mom's face:

> *"How DARE you walk out of my sermon?!? Who do you think you are?? You are condemning your children to Hell with your actions!"*

(Wrong move, man! Have you met my mom? Father Delaney, meet Marilyn Maria Marguerite Meyer Mann. She takes shit from no one; and you're about to find out!)

Without missing a beat, Mom grabbed Delaney by the shoulders, spun him 180 degrees, stuck her foot right in his ass, and kicked him off our porch! Delaney stumbled down the three steps, turned around with a stunned look on his face, and Mom unleashed her wrath:

> *"You miserable old son-of-a-bitch! If you ever step foot on my property and talk to me that way, you'll get worse!"*

And, with that, she marched back into the house, and slammed the door. I didn't know whether to tell her how cool that was or run and hide. There may have been some residual anger left, and I didn't want to suffer Friendly Fire.

Mom never took us back to St. Bridget's for services, again. And, the world didn't end. We never heard from Father Delaney, or anyone else from the church, ever again.

Years later, when I was an adult, and my son, Nick, was ready to attend school, Sue and I enrolled him at St. Bridget's. Father Delaney was long gone, and Father Joe Donnelly was there. Father Joe is a truly great man. Sister Catherine was the Principal at the time, and Nick loved it…

…and, we all went back to church.

BONUS STORY #2
Done in by the Ghost of Louisa May Alcott

I don't know how I had forgotten about this story, while writing The Delmont Street Gang. Maybe, I had blocked it out as a traumatic memory.

One weekend, toward the end of my fifth-grade year at Bentley Elementary School, Mom and Dad took us to Massachusetts, to visit the sights of the American Revolution. You know. Boston, Lexington and Concord? The "Shot Heard 'Round the World"? Stuff like that. They were always exposing us to history or culture, whether we liked it, or not!

It was during this trip that Jessie insisted that we visit the home of the renowned author of Little Women, Louisa May Alcott. Now, for an eleven-year-old boy, this tour meant less-than-nothing to me. I wouldn't be caught dead reading such a book! And, if the gang had found out that I had, I would probably be hung by my underwear on the nearest telephone pole.

242

So, bored to tears, and waiting with Dad and Claudia for Jessie and mom to complete the tour of the Alcott homestead, I looked for other things to occupy my time. Along the right side of the house was a dirt road. To the right of the dirt road was a small, tree-covered hill. There, on one of the trees closest to the road, I found a vine. I soon found out that it was a perfect "Tarzan Swing"; it was long and strong and could hold my weight. While grasping the vine, and not giving thought to the possible peril I might inflict upon myself, I leapt into space, and swung several feet over the dirt road, and back again. Now, this was cool!

Over the next several minutes, a small crowd would gather, with many of the spectators "ooh-ing and ahh-ing" and laughing. Dad was reminding me to be careful. Finally, Mom and Jessie exited the tour, and saw me acting like the loony I was. Mom laughed; Jessie was disgusted at the spectacle that was her stupid, little brother.

Finally, it was time to pile into the Mann Family station wagon, for the long ride back to Manchester. As usual, I climbed into the back of the vehicle, to stretch out. I eventually dozed off.

It was over the course of the next few hours that I started to feel strange; a little itchy. I didn't think much of it, thinking it was just the result of dirt and sweat that any kid my age might encounter.

When we finally arrived home, we all piled out of the car, and Mom told use to get washed-up, and ready for bed. I took my bath, put on my jammies, and climbed into bed for a good night's sleep. I drifted away to "Slumberland" thinking about the upcoming field trip to Mystic Seaport that my class would be taking in the next few days, and the fun we would have, missing a full-day of school.

A few hours later, I woke up. I was itching all over. And, I mean a BAAAAAAAD itching; my arms, my legs, my crotch, EVERYWHERE! I couldn't take it anymore. I climbed out of bed and put on my glasses. But they didn't fit right. What was *that* about? I walked downstairs, to find Mom, who was in the dining room, working on her sewing machine.

"Mom, something's wrong. I don't feel right."

"What do you mean, you don't feel… OH MY GAWWWWWD! IRVING!! GET DOWN HERE!!!"

Dad plowed down the stairs, took one look at me, and said *"Oh shit!"*

There I stood, in all my glory, eyes swollen shut, and hundreds of welts all over my body! The vine on which I was swinging…?

POISON SUMAC!

Over the next several days, I was on lockdown. I couldn't go to school; and forget about the field trip. It was a constant battle involving gallons of pink calamine lotion, baking soda baths, and sleepless nights. I was a mess. It was disgusting!

The last thing I remember about this experience was me, looking out our front door, watching the convoy of school busses passing by my house on their way to the much-anticipated field trip, while I sobbed.

Bonus Story #3
A Connecticut Christmas Story

My son Nick was a little guy; probably no more than five or six. It was a couple of weeks before the "Big Day", and he was having difficulty finding the Christmas spirit. In short, he was being a little grumpy.

I tried to reason with him, In the most-fatherly way, by telling him that Santa would soon be here, and he had better be on his best behavior, or Santa may not visit our house.

In all the defiance he could muster, Nick courageously proclaimed, *"I don't care!"*

"Oh really? Okay, let's just give him a call."

I picked up the phone and dialed the one person I knew who could seamlessly impersonate Jolly Old Saint Nick on the spot, Jonathan Adams.

"Hello Santa? This is Nicholas Mann's dad. Nick is not being a very good boy, and I thought you'd like to speak with him."

"Ho Ho Ho! Well, put him on the phone!"

Nick's eyes opened wide, and the look of fear took over. I handed him the phone and, with a trembling hand, he held the receiver to his ear:

"H...h...hello Santa?"

For the next several minutes, Nick mostly listened in wonderment, and uttered several "uh-huhs" and various one-word answers, totally engrossed in the wisdom of this magical purveyor of presents.

Finally, the conversation wound down:

"Okay Santa, I will. I promise."

And then, Nick offered one last parting sentiment, with the innocence only a child could offer:

"Bye Santa. I love you."

I felt the emotion welling up inside, as my boy looked up at me, and handed over the phone.

Jon had come through for me, in a big way. Not only had he changed Nick's holiday spirit, he gave us a Christmas memory we will always cherish.

I wanted to thank him profusely but had to continue the charade in front of my son. So, I simply said:

"Thank you so much, Santa. We'll see you on Christmas Eve!"

And, as if ordained to continue in this magical role, Jon simply said:

"Ho Ho Ho! Fuck you!" and hung up the phone.

God bless us, everyone!

Made in the USA
Middletown, DE
15 November 2020

24115281R10139